Time Travels

*Stories from a remarkable
50-year journey*

By Catherine Deveney

1965 50 2015

H I E
Highlands and Islands Enterprise
Iomairt na Gàidhealtachd 's nan Eilean

Fans at Belladrum Festival 2013

1965 50 2015

H I E
Highlands and Islands Enterprise
Iomairt na Gàidhealtachd 's nan Eilean

Contents

PREFACE/RO-RÀDH

Professor Lorne Crerar,
Chairman,
Highlands and Islands Enterprise

The creation of the Highlands and Islands Development Board (HIDB) in 1965 was a bold step with far-reaching consequences. The world today is a very different place, and so is the Highlands and Islands. However the unique economic and community development remit which has defined HIDB and its successor Highlands and Islands Enterprise (HIE), is as relevant today as it was back then.

As Chairman of HIE, it is my privilege to travel all around this beautiful region, meeting some remarkable people, and seeing for myself the fruits of 50 years of progress. What has been achieved here is a transformation. A region which, half a century ago, seemed trapped in a downward spiral is now one of the most prosperous parts of Scotland. Where the challenge of 1965 was to halt and reverse decline, in the 21st century, it is to sustain progress across most of the region, and to extend its benefits to those areas which have not, as yet, advanced as strongly.

The transformation of the Highlands and Islands has been achieved by many individuals, and many organisations. At its heart, however, has been Highlands and Islands Enterprise and its forerunner, and it is to all those who have contributed to the work of these organisations that I wish to dedicate this book. It is my greatest hope that HIE will remain active at the heart of the Highlands and Islands, continuing to address the region's economic opportunities and challenges with passion, creativity and perseverance, for generations to come.

Bha cruthachadh Bòrd Leasachaidh na Gàidhealtachd is nan Eilean (HIDB) an 1965 na cheum mòr, dàna; ceum a bha le iomadh buaidh na lùib. Tha saoghal là an-diugh gu tur eadar-dhealaichte an taca ri 1965, agus tha an aon rud fìor mun Ghàidhealtachd is na h-Eileanan. A dh'aindheoin seo, bha an t-adhbhar airson HIDB a bhith ann a cheart cho iomchaidh dha Iomairt na Gàidhealtachd is nan Eilean (HIE) san là an-diugh.

Mar Chathraiche HIE, tha e air a bhith na urram dhomh a dhol timcheall na sgìre àlainn seo, a' coinneachadh dhaoine iongantach, a' faicinn buaidh leth-cheud bliadhna de dh'adhartas. 'S e mòr-atharrachadh a chunnacas an seo, an sgìre a bha, leth-cheud bliadhna air ais, a' sìor chrìonadh ach a tha a-nise am measg nan sgìrean as beartaiche an Alba. Ged a b' èiginn dha HIDB an 1965 dèiligeadh ris a' chrìonadh agus obair chum fàs,'s e tha romhainn san 21d linn ach adhartas a chumail a' dol air feadh na sgìre, leis na buannachdan gan shìneadh a-mach chun nan ceàrnaidhean nach eil air an uiread dhiubh fhaicinn gu seo.

Thàinig an leasachadh mòr seo ri linn obair mòran daoine is bhuidhnean. Aig cridhe na h-obrach, tha Iomairt na Gàidhealtachd is nan Eilean agus HIDB roimhpe agus tha mi airson is gum bi an leabhar seo na chomharrachadh air obair nam buidhnean seo. 'S e mo rùn gun cùm HIE a' dol ag obair aig cridhe obrach leasachaidh na sgìre, a' dèiligeadh ri cothroman is dùbhlain gu h-innleachdach, dealasach, dìcheallach fad ghinealaichean mòra fhathast.

Flying from North Ronaldsay to Kirkwall, Orkney.

FOREWORD/FACAL-TOISICH

Alex Paterson,
Chief Executive,
Highlands and Islands Enterprise

When the initial group of just six employees of the new Highlands and Islands Development Board first sat at their desks on 1 November, 1965, they must surely have been aware of the scale of the challenge laid out before them. This was the start of a self-described 'experiment' to tackle 'the Highland problem' – a seemingly unstoppable downward spiral affecting the whole regional economy. Fifty years on, with population rising, unemployment low, confident and resilient communities, and a broader range of industries than ever before, that experiment must be judged a success.

In the spring of 2015, Highlands and Islands Enterprise asked young people their views of the region, and their aspirations for its future. Almost 4,500 people aged 15 to 30 took part and the results were hugely encouraging. They told us the range of opportunities, quality of life, and strong community links were all positive factors in encouraging growing numbers of young people to want to live here.

Perhaps it isn't hard to see why. The Highlands and Islands of Scotland is famed worldwide for its natural beauty, culture and history. It is also one of Europe's most dynamic and successful regions, with a diverse and thriving economy, where community-led development has taken root, arguably more significantly than anywhere else. From Shetland to Argyll, and from the Outer Hebrides to Moray, examples of flourishing and ambitious businesses, social enterprises, communities and individuals abound.

Take the world-leading European Marine Energy Centre in Orkney, the creative industries cluster centred around Mareel in Shetland, the unique Harris Tweed industry in the Outer Hebrides, Gaelic higher education at Sabhal Mòr Ostaig UHI on Skye, the UK's outdoor capital in Lochaber, pioneering marine science research in Argyll, the Scottish-based, internationally-feted food companies in Moray, leading IT and life science businesses in the Inner Moray Firth… the dynamism of this region is evident everywhere you look. That's even before we consider that the Highlands and Islands produces the world's most famous whiskies, and that its ability to attract hundreds of thousands of tourists every year continues to grow.

It seemed fitting, therefore, for Highlands and Islands Enterprise, which succeeded the former HIDB in 1991, to produce a publication to mark our joint golden anniversary. But what kind of book should it be? To catalogue all the significant events of the past 50 years in the Highlands and Islands, or even to describe the current range of initiatives with which the development agency is now involved across the region, would require many more thousands of words than are written here. Instead, we decided to capture something of the *spirit* of the Highlands and Islands, as expressed through the images of the region and the words of its people.

To accomplish this, we asked award-winning journalist and author Catherine Deveney, who lives in Ross-shire, to make a series of journeys across the Highlands and Islands, speak to a range of local people about their experience of living and working here, and share her own observations from these travels. The result is the book you are now reading.

Whatever you know about the Highlands and Islands already, I hope you will find plenty in the pages ahead to interest, entertain and surprise you – and perhaps to share with others to help tell the story of our region's past and present, and join us in shaping its future.

Nuair a shuidhe sianar luchd-obrach HIDB shìos aig na deasgaichean aca air 1 Samhain 1965, feumaidh gun robh beachd aca dè meud na h-obrach mòire a bha romhpa. B' e seo toiseach-tòiseachaidh air an 'experiment' airson dèiligeadh ris an 'Highland problem' – crìonadh nach gabhadh stad a bha a' toirt buaidh air eaconamaidh na sgìre gu lèir. Leth-cheud bliadhna air adhart, leis an àireimh-shluaigh a' fàs, cion-cosnaidh ìosal, coimhearsnachdan misneachail 's seasmhach, agus farsaingeachd mhòr ghnìomhachasan nach fhacas roimhe, faodar a chantainn gun do shoirbhich leis an 'experiment'.

As t-earrach 2015, chuir HIE ceistean air daoine òga na sgìre, air na bha iad airson fhaicinn a' tachairt san àm ri teachd. Fhuaireas freagairtean air ais bho, cha mhòr, 4,500 duine eadar 15-30 le misneachd gu leòr ri fhaighinn às na toraidhean. Thuirt iad rinn gun robh farsaingeachd chothroman, càileachd beatha, agus ceanglaichean làidir coimhearsnachd uile a' toirt air barrachd dhaoine òga miannachadh fuireach sa sgìre.

Tha tàlaidheachd na sgìre furasta gu leòr a thuigse. Tha cliù mhòr aig a' Ghàidhealtachd air feadh an t-saoghail mar àite breagha le beartas cultair is eachdraidh. 'S i cuideachd sgìre a tha dìoghrasach is soirbheachail, le eaconamaidh air leth fallain le iomadh seòrsa ghnìomhachas a' dol, agus na sgìre sa bheil leasachadh fo stiùir na coimhearsnachd le freumhaichean a tha dha-rìribh domhainn. Bho Shealtainn gu Earra-Ghàidheal, na h-Eileanan Siar gu Moireabh, tha eisimpleirean de shoirbheachas am measg chompanaidhean, iomairtean sòisealta, choimhearsnachdan agus dhaoine fa leth ri fhaicinn fad is farsaing.

Feuch Ionad Cumhachd Mara na h-Eòrpa an Arcaibh, cruinneachadh nan gnìomhachasan cruthachail timcheall air Mareel an Sealtainn, gnìomhachas Clò na Hearadh an Leòdhas 's na Hearadh, Foghlam Gàidhlig aig àird-ìre aig Sabhal Mòr Ostaig UHI, cliù mhòr Loch Abar 'son nan spòrs a-muigh, rannsachadh adhartach air na saidheansan mara an Earra-Ghàidheal, companaidhean-bidhe Mhoireibh a tha ainmeil air feadh an t-saoghail, companaidhean IT 's nan saidheansan beatha timcheall Inbhir Nis… tha spiorad dealasach na sgire ri fhaicinn air feadh na Gàidhealtachd is nan Eilean. Tha sin mas toir sinn guth air na h-uisgeachan-beatha as ainmeil air an t-saoghal, agus gu bheil iad a' tàladh mhìltean mòra de luchd-turais gach bliadhna.

Cha robh e ach iomchaidh, mar seo, gun dèanamh HIE, a thàinig an àite HIDB an 1991, leabhar a' comharrachadh 50 bliadhna. Ach dè seòrsa leabhar bu chòir a bhiodh ann? Airson iomradh a thoirt air gach leasachadh thar 50 bliadhna, no eadhon gus sgrìobhadh air an fharsaingeachd mhòir iomairtean sa bheil sinn an sàs an-dràsta, dh'fheumadh leabhar mòr tomadach a sgrìobhadh. Seach seo a dhèanamh, chuir sinn romhainn rud a chur ann an clò stèidhte air *spiorad* na Gàidhealtachd is nan Eilean; ga thoirt seachad tro dhealbhan agus tro fhacail muinntir na sgìre.

Dh'iarr sinn air an sgrìobhadair Catherine Deveney, a tha a' fuireach an Siorrachd Rois, a dhol air cuairt timcheall na Gàidhealtachd is nan Eilean agus a bhruidhinn ri muinntir nan diofar àiteachan mum bheatha aca ag obair agus a' gabhail còmhnaidh sa sgìre. 'S e an leabhar seo toradh nan cuairtean is còmhraidhean sin.

Eadar gu bheil eòlas agaibh air a' Ghàidhealtachd is nach eil, tha mi an dòchas gum faigh sibh rudan inntinneach, iongantach, àraid sa leabhar seo, ach am faigh sibh cothrom air faighinn a-mach mu eachdraidh obair-leasachaidh sa sgìre, agus cothrom air a dhol an sàs san obair seo thar nam bliadhnachan a tha romhainn.

INTRODUCTION

Catherine Deveney,
Author

It was not love at first sight. It was a slow burn affair, igniting only after a period of teenage indifference. For long enough, I spurned the object of my future affections cruelly, little guessing that one day I'd be hooked and humbled. Each year, I snapped my case shut with a sigh before Highland holidays, a surly, city-slicker, what-no-shops, sigh of frustration that we were leaving Glasgow for the land of moors and heather again. I painted 'Pouting Pink' on my lips, hobbled painfully across rocky ground in four inch heels, and watched the rain drumming on the window panes of holiday homes that housed china cups in dressers and smelled vaguely of damp. There was no TV, though the kind man next door invited us in to watch Scotland play on a grainy picture that looked like there was a July snow storm hovering over Hampden Park. They lost anyway.

How could I know that one day, I'd be seduced by the Highlands and Islands before I even realised I was being wooed? The fire of its sunsets, the gentleness of its dawns, the thunder of its seas and waterfalls. How could I know that its spirit would inveigle its way gradually, insidiously, inside me, that its landscape would creep into my novels when I wasn't looking, that its light and space and colour would fill a place inside that nowhere else could? After all, I was the one of six children who didn't want to go there. The one who ended up living here. But looking back perhaps there were signs of a flirtation that would deepen. Memories like delicate glass baubles line my mind… moments trapped inside…

Five years old. A fisherman's cottage in Catacol, Arran, facing the sea. The crunch of gravel stones on the garden path. A hedge of red fuchsia spilling over the gate. The buzz of bees. The feel of holiday shoes, Woolworths sneakers, on my feet. The creak of the latch on the gate, the beach beckoning, the smell of seaweed and brine, moss peeking through the cracks on the rocks, the feel of tiny flounders flicking between my toes in rock pools. But above all the feeling of fantasy; the sense that this was a world set apart. It was the realisation that not everywhere was constructed in concrete and glass, or filled with exhaust fumes, that not all playgrounds involved cemeteries, or crumbling "haunted" houses where we played amongst the rubble, that not every minute, everywhere, was filled with noise. To a city child who lived in a flat, there was a kind of magic in seeing the sea from your bedroom, in simply crossing a road to jump directly onto a rocky shore. That close. That real. That enchanting.

Catacol cottages, Arran

It's remarkable how quickly you become associated with, have an affinity with, this area. You find yourself going in to bat for the Highlands and Islands.

Alex Paterson,
HIE Chief Executive, 2010 to present

Later, the annual summer retreat from Glasgow for the family holiday involved Arisaig, then Lower Breakish, near Broadford, on the Isle of Skye. On Skye, I applied a thicker layer of 'Pouting Pink' for the admired-from-a-distance student barman up from Glasgow. I stayed in a croft house that despite my snotty, city-girl protestations offered a haven of peace, a place where my bedroom was decorated in sunshine lemon and where you didn't dare open the windows at night or the sherbet walls would turn black with midges. A place with an upstairs bench seat that ran right along the window where I curled up and read a book a day, listened to the mysterious screeches of wildlife in the night, and woke to the harsh, grating call of the corncrake that lived somewhere at the bottom of the croft.

Food was different from the city. On Arran, there were fresh rolls from the local bakery while groceries and butcher meat came in vans. On Skye, there was Orkney Cheese and Walkers Strathspey fruitcake, but you had to check the date on the packets and finding an apple without a wrinkle was a challenge. Shops had a tendency to look like the set for a 1970s sitcom.

Supplies were at the mercy of the railways, seas and increasingly the roads, the unpredictability of the weather, and the vagaries of the boats to the islands. The A9, the road that runs from the central belt all the way to Thurso was a 300-mile long artery that pumped supplies through the veins of the Highlands. But it was slow. The road has been modernised over the years, knocking hours off journey times, and it will be even further transformed in future when the entire length of it becomes dual carriageway.

Different days. Once I merely visited; now I live and work in the Highlands. It was purely accident that I ended up here. Or perhaps 'serendipity' is a nicer word, capturing as it does the good fortune of that happenstance. I applied all over Scotland in the 1980s for my first post teaching English and Drama. Inverness offered the only vacancy and interview. I travelled up from Glasgow by train, emerging into Station Square with no real idea of where I was, and got the job.

Then came the switch to journalism. I spent years working for an Edinburgh based newspaper as a feature writer and celebrity interviewer. In the decade from the late 1990s, I talked to famous people, usually in London, and readers thought I was based there, or at least that I travelled from the central belt. Actually, I was in the middle of a sheep field on a plot on a Black Isle farm. The area in which I could barely get a TV picture in my childhood now offered broadband, wifi, mobile phones, and flights to London.

Black Isle

When I look at photograph albums, I almost can't believe I was there at the time. It looks like a completely different age. Communications were fundamentally different. I remember Edinburgh was a day's journey to get to the ferry – there was no Forth Road Bridge – and you had to wait hours for that ferry. Now you can go there and back in a day. Communication has fundamentally changed the prospects of the area.

Sir Fraser Morrison,
HIE Chairman, 1992-1998

I am not saying it was easy. It wasn't. But it was possible if you wanted the Highland lifestyle enough. How did this transformation come about? It began 50 years ago, in 1965, when Willie Ross, then Secretary of State for Scotland in Harold Wilson's Labour government, gave an important speech. Introducing the establishment of one of Europe's first ever development agencies, the Highlands and Islands Development Board (HIDB), Ross told MPs in the Westminster parliament, "For two hundred years the Highlander has been the man on Scotland's conscience."

What did Ross mean? The Highlands had a turbulent history that included the Clearances, mass emigration, and the ruthless demolition of its language and culture. Its history, but also its geography, meant the area faced considerable, distinctive challenges and Ross was acknowledging that the Highlander had been unfairly abandoned for generations to deal with those challenges alone. Its remote nature which made communication and travel difficult. Its ageing, falling population. Its fragile economy, high unemployment rate and low wages.

The village of Lochcarron with the snow capped
Applecross mountains beyond

Its over-reliance on the traditional industries of crofting, fishing and farming and the lack of infrastructure for industry and new technology. Its lack of modern, affordable housing. The Highlands and Islands accounts for more than half of Scotland's land mass but just 8% of the country's population. Ross knew that the area was on the brink of steep and terminal decline.

HIDB's role, Ross said, was twofold. The first task was to, "assist the people of the Highlands and Islands to improve their economic and social conditions". The second was to, "enable the Highlands and Islands to play a more effective part in the economic and social development of the nation". Crucially these two tasks did not just contain an economic remit but also a social one. HIDB, in other words, was charged with establishing the kinds of businesses, infrastructure, and community spirit that created both economic and social opportunity. If HIDB could grow businesses, it would create living and working opportunities in the Highlands and Islands. If it could strengthen communities, it would make them viable again, offering people

I think the 70s in Inverness were the start of an era. Suddenly, it was no longer a backwater. You could see the tide turning. There were opportunities. Things were beginning to improve.

Sandy Cumming,
HIE Chief Executive, 2000-2010

HIE and HIDB have had to really listen to the people, have had to be brave, have needed the ability to take risks and back some of the most apparently crazy ideas. Norfrost were turned down the first time they applied when they said they were going to build freezers in Caithness. You can't be serious. It's not possible. They proved us wrong, and went on to become a global name, employing up to 400 people for over 30 years. You need that attitude.

Sandy Cumming,
HIE Chief Executive, 2000-2010

the opportunity to make a life in one of the most beautiful parts of the country.

The strategy worked. By 1971, the first recorded growth in Highlands and Islands population in a century was being reported in the census and that rise has continued over the decades since.
But it was not the work of HIDB alone. It was also the work of the many partners that HIDB has forged relationships with. Public partners like the region's seven local authorities, Creative Scotland and the University of the Highlands and Islands, but also private partners who were prepared to bring substantial inward investment to a fragile area. Then, of course, there was the European Union whose financial contribution through Objective 1 money for Europe's most deprived areas transformed infrastructure throughout the region supporting civil engineering projects like roads and harbours, but also the development of communications technology in the area.

In the early days, HIDB concentrated on the areas of employment traditionally associated with the Highlands and Islands: fishing, farming and crofting with a growing emphasis on tourism. But as time went by, it became more daring, more innovative and more imaginative. As you will read in the chapters that follow, over the years HIDB, and its successor Highlands and Islands Enterprise, attracted major international investment by companies like LifeScan in Inverness; helped establish the University of the Highlands and Islands; supported Premier League Football; and contributed to the development of internationally renowned green energy projects like the European Marine Energy Centre and the Meygen tidal energy project. It also ploughed money into sustaining communities in fragile areas, sometimes as straightforwardly as building a community hall to support village activities. Fifty years after HIDB was established, large parts of the area are now thriving economically and socially, with a lower unemployment rate than the Scottish average.

Shetland Folk Festival

You have to combine economic and social development. It's not about running them separately; it's running them together. HIDB was set up with a unique remit and consistency of approach is really important. You have to have continuity. This development agency has had broadly the same mandate for 50 years.

Alex Paterson,
HIE Chief Executive, 2010 to present

Being chairman of HIE is one of the best jobs on the planet. It's a very positive, purposeful organisation and it's nice to be part of something that is truly delivering. An organisation that has been in-built into the culture for 50 years has an enormous opportunity.

Lorne Crerar,
HIE Chairman, 2012 to present

In 1991, when it was 25 years old, HIDB became Highlands and Islands Enterprise (HIE). The structure of the organisation changed and a network of 10 local enterprise companies (LECs) were formed to support its work in different locations in the region. Providing front-line assistance, guidance and advice to individual people, community groups and businesses, the LECs were truly devolved organisations, managed by local boards. The board members from a range of backgrounds gave their time freely in order to contribute to the economic development of their local areas. This would strengthen local activity but initially there was a worry that the emphasis would now be solely on business. The fears were unfounded. None of the HIDB social powers were removed from its successor and in fact, in the second 25 years of the development agency's existence, its community work has strengthened. HIE has played a critical role in providing support to communities not just through strengthening communications and internet connectivity, but in fundamental ways such as enabling them to purchase, own and administer their own lands through the Scottish Land Fund.

HIE is a robust organisation. Like any public body it has had its share of criticism over the years. Rightly so – it administers public money and accountability is therefore critical. But there would be few who would argue that the organisation has not been an overwhelmingly positive one in the regeneration of the Highlands and Islands.

When you travel round the region, you might easily miss the small plaques on so many walls, on so many business foyers, public buildings and institutions, indicating that HIE has supported that particular venture. This book does the work of those plaques. The pages that follow are not a definitive guide to the entire Highlands and Islands. It is too vast an area for that. They are simply representations, examples of key areas of the region, places where HIDB and HIE made a contribution, made a difference, in the last fifty years. The people who have benefited talk in their own words, their own voices.

Coastline to the east of Hopeman, Moray

Nobody would deny corporate mistakes. There is no attempt to cover HIE's failed investments: the collapsed bulb growing business on Uist, or the controversial plans, never fulfilled, for a petrochemical plant at Invergordon. Then there's the former local enterprise company Chief Executive who tells of backing a small plane business on the islands. The plane physically disappeared after a year… never to return. It's part of the story. A development agency has to exercise appropriate caution and judgment, but it can't simply back those ventures that are guaranteed successes and will happen anyway. Risk – calculated risk – is part of its business. It's why it exists.

As a child, I loved that first holiday home on Arran with its exotic, glassy eyed stag's head in the porch. Ernie we called him. It was a house of dreams and it seemed enormous. We ran through it, held treasure hunts in its vastness, pushed back chairs and danced in the dining room. A few years ago, I returned for the first time since childhood. It wasn't available to rent for the weekend I was there but I was allowed to see inside. It was tiny. A tiny fisherman's cottage. How did we all fit in, the eight of us? In the dining room, I saw my late father in the chair where I danced on a postage stamp floor and marvelled at the mendacity of memory.

So many ghosts. Times change. Standards change. You can't see the past through the eyes of the present. But 'then' exists in layers inside 'now'. We are what we are because of our experiences. It has been the challenge for HIDB and HIE to recognise and protect the special quality of this area's past while developing its future. Not to change it beyond recognition, nor to preserve it in dust sheets, but to breathe new life into it by making it viable. That economic and social viability has enabled incomers like me to use a very special word to describe the Highlands and Islands: home.

Beach at Arisaig

Ross-shire to Skye

I have been lucky enough to travel the world, but the Highlands and Islands is the most beautiful place on the planet. It is. So varied, so wonderful… I have a very busy life and when I get to Glen Docherty which is the entrance to Loch Maree, it's a kind of Brigadoon moment for me. I leave my other world behind and enter a new one.

Lorne Crerar,
HIE Chairman, 2012 to present

In the car park at the village of Broadford, on the Isle of Skye, rain is hammering on the car roof with all the rhythm and ferocity of regimental drums. There's barely a seat to be had in Café Sia, where the coffee machine hisses busily and the smell of wood-fired pizzas drifts out into the damp atmosphere. Outside the steamy windows, the island is temporarily washed of colour, grey skies and grey sea merging into one, entire hills hidden in the iron hues of a spring downpour. Eilean a Cheò; Isle of Mist.

The two-and-a-half-hour journey from Ross-shire has been sunshine and showers, winding through the village of Achnasheen before climbing high into the hills above Loch Carron. The road then drops from Strome Ferry past the picturesque village of Plockton which nestles securely in a horse-shoe shaped bay – complete with exotic palm trees –

to Kyle of Lochalsh. It's close to heaven at the height of those hills, the view plunging into lochs, soaring into sky and mountain peaks, and even in the showers, the summer hills are lit by a blaze of broom and gorse that illuminates the landscape like sunlight.

At Kyle of Lochalsh, the Skye Bridge looms, arcing from the mainland to the island. The bridge opened as a toll bridge in 1995 but after much controversy and political lobbying, the tolls were dropped.

The economic benefits are obvious: tourists now stream across to the island free of charge, making it hard at times in summer to find a restaurant table in Skye's biggest town, Portree. Ferries also operate from other Skye ports, creating a network both to the mainland and to other islands of the Outer Hebrides: Armadale to Mallaig; Uig to Tarbert on Harris; and Uig to Lochmaddy on North Uist.

Broadford is just eight miles into Skye from the bridge. As the rain hammers down, tourists run to Café Sia, umbrellas dripping, still wanting to be here in this bustling haven despite the deluge. Craft shops and cafés, workshops and galleries pay testimony to an island that has seen its population rise from around 7,000 in 1965 when HIDB was formed, to over 10,000 in the 2011 census. Even today, in the torrential rain, you can understand the attraction.

The Skye Bridge over Loch Alsh

I grew up in Duror, south of Ballachulish and went to Oban High School. At that time, you took it for granted that if you had success, you would go off to university and never come back. If you were going to get on, you got out. Three or four good Highers and a grant were the equivalent of the emigrant ship. That lack of belief in the area was very important.

Jim Hunter,
HIE Chairman, 1998-2004

Waterstein Head and Moonen Bay,
Isle of Skye

The morning after the night before, Skye is like a different island: washed clean, refreshed, the gently muted shades of a watercolour painting washing across the landscape. Then, as the sun intensifies, there's a sparkle, a vibrancy, as the soft blues and green of the hills and sea, the lavenders of the heather, become suddenly richer and more vivid.

On the road from Broadford to Portree, the undulating road rises and dips against a backdrop of triangular peaked mountains. Waterfalls gush down sheer rockface round one bend, while a body of moorland rolls in sensuous curves into the horizon round another. Something here feels ancient and spiritual, a glimpse of heaven, a taste of eternity.

"You can't eat scenery."

So said the mother of Campbell Grant, Managing Director of Sitekit Ltd, a company that produces health software. Campbell is recalling his mother's words with a smile as we sit on black leather sofas in an informal back office on a small industrial estate on the outskirts of Portree. A vase of fresh flowers brightens the space. Campbell had told his mother he wanted to return to Skye after studying engineering in Glasgow and working in Aberdeen. "I didn't pay for you to go to university just to come back here!" she told him.

To Campbell's mother's generation, both the island and its language were a dead end. She wanted more for her children. She was a Gaelic speaker but told her son, who went to school in Portree, not to bother with that old stuff. "You'll take French," she told him. Campbell never learned Gaelic but now his children speak the language of their grandparents having received Gaelic medium education, and his daughter is now teaching it. Times have changed here.

> *The job of an economic development agency is not to ensure that all businesses necessarily last forever, but that there is a steady flow of businesses that help bring prosperity to every part of the region.*
>
> **Willy Roe,**
> HIE Chairman, 2004-2012

For a start, the island hosts Sabhal Mòr Ostaig, the Gaelic college which now plays a central role in the University of the Highlands and Islands as the national centre for the Gaelic language, and which has been instrumental in transforming not just the cultural and economic landscape of Skye, but of many other parts of the Highlands and Islands.

Campbell has another visitor when I call by. Malcolm Henry, his close friend since schooldays, has dropped in for a chat. Sometimes, when Campbell needs a temporary, freelance member of staff, Malcolm helps him out. They have both run businesses on the island over the years and have seen confidence in the area grow. "We were part of the first generation who were not just trying to get away," says Campbell. "If you had any ambition, you weren't meant to stay here," agrees Malcolm.

But, says Campbell, "HIDB helped change that attitude." He was called 'Bambi' at school and he had big ambitions that fitted with the new surge of confidence in his area. "Together, we used to build radio controlled planes and I'd stick labels on them that said, 'Made in Scotland by Bambi Engineering'. I said one day, I'll build real planes." He didn't, but Malcolm built real boats, establishing a business with the assistance of a grant from HIDB. It didn't last forever, his business, but it contributed to the local economy for 20 years which is significant in an economically challenging area.

So why the name Bambi? "Bambi… Campbell," says Campbell, implying it was just childish mispronunciation. "It was really because he was his mother's little dear!" scoffs Malcolm.

Campbell smiles wryly. He is friendly, welcoming but with that sharp, sardonic humour so typical of the Islands. 'Well now, you're a smart city person', his tone seems to imply, 'and I'm just a country bumpkin'. But Campbell has taken Sitekit through several different incarnations since its inception in 1989. It employs around 25 people locally, a significant number in a rural community.

The business started out specialising in computer control systems in the energy sector. One of Campbell's early contracts involved redesigning the system measuring the oil flow from Sullom Voe, which at the time represented a significant contribution to Britain's balance of payments. Being out with the measurements by even 0.1% would have cost the country dearly. "Any slight miscalculation would have cost millions of pounds a day," laughs Campbell insouciantly. "And the entire project," he adds with relish, "was directed from a Portakabin on a croft in the Braes area of Skye."

Campbell and Malcolm have watched the transformation on Skye, the growth in both population and confidence. "HIE has grown the economic base," says Campbell. "We are no longer dependent on agriculture, fisheries and forestry as we once were. It has created diversity and had a significant impact." Along with the West Highland Free Press, adds Malcolm. But how can a newspaper affect economics? It affected self-belief, both men agree. "In the early 70s these young guys came up from Dundee University and set up a radical local paper," says Malcolm, "and they started all sorts of conversations, challenged authority, affected confidence."

The West Highland Free Press became a well-respected, campaigning voice of the Highlands and Islands that held public bodies, including HIDB and HIE, to account. They constantly championed the needs of the most rural parts of the region. "They changed the traditional view," says Campbell. "They showed you can do much more here."

Despite his location, Campbell was quick to spot the potential of the world wide web and Sitekit subsequently evolved into a business that developed websites for businesses. The area has significant broadband issues which are currently being addressed by HIE. Those problems will be solved in the future but how did he establish a high-tech web business from a remote island in the first place? "We like a challenge," he says. "It's not all about location and services. You need people with ideas and the perseverance to realise them." The company rents space on 'the cloud' and stores their data there.

Campbell Grant, Managing Director of Sitekit Ltd

The most recent transformation for Sitekit came when it began developing software for a number of key economic sectors. In 2010, a strategic decision was taken to focus on software for health. "We want to turn it from a national sickness service to a national wellness service, by empowering people" says Campbell. "Most people spend more on an MOT for their car than they do on their own bodies. They just wait until they break down. We want to support people to manage long-term conditions with better access to their own health information."

Sitekit now has offices in Oxford, Cambridge and Edinburgh and employs a total of 36 staff. People always assume Skye is the little satellite office. They are amazed when Campbell tells them it's the headquarters, even if it means he has to travel a lot. "You can produce software here, but to sell it, you need to go south." Is the travel worth it? "Absolutely. Our lifestyle here is not negotiable. Kirsty (his wife) and I are here and the business has to deal with that."

It seems an irrelevant question when you stand in Skye and look out at the distant hills, watch the sunlight streaming across jewelled water. But what makes living here special? "It's the sense of identity," says Campbell. "To be a 'Sgitheanach' – to 'come from Skye'. I wanted my children to have that sense of identity too. So I smiled inside, when my son introduced himself to his new university flatmates with "Hi, I'm Angus from Skye". You are part of a community and it's so valuable if you have experienced it. You don't have to lock doors. You know your neighbours. The teachers who are teaching my children taught me. You can't put a price on that. And then there's the landscape…"

Live in the city? Not on your life. Why would he? In terms of lifestyle, what could the city possibly offer in comparison to this? And in terms of business, he knows what's needed to make it work for him here. "Business training and raising ambitions for island entrepreneurs is key," he says. "You have to raise ambition if you want to be successful in business – it's a global village now and everything is competitive. So we are trying to be the best in the world at what we do."

The view across Loch Scavaig
from Elgol to the Black Cuillin

The Caledonian MacBrayne ferry sailing from the tiny island of Raasay is steaming across the calm waters of the Sound of Raasay towards Sconser, half way between Portree and Broadford. The crisp white, red and black livery of the ferry company is a familiar site round the Highlands and Islands, maintaining vital links for remote communities. On board is Roger Hutchinson, a writer and journalist from the north of England who has lived on Skye, then Raasay, for almost 40 years. Campbell and Malcolm's comments about the importance of the West Highland Free Press make it important to meet one of the paper's key voices over the last four decades. Roger is already on the slipway when my car turns into the ferry car park, a warm, engaging figure with a broad smile and a whole-hearted husky laugh that tells a tale of the roll-up fags in his pocket.

Roger has been a radical voice on the West Highland Free Press since the 1970s. The paper that so inspired the young Campbell and Malcolm to take confidence in their community, their heritage and their language, to demand rather than beg, has been an influential critic of HIDB and then HIE over the years. Rightly so. They have held decisions up to the light for scrutiny and made the publicly-funded organisations accountable for their investments.

Within minutes of meeting, the interior of the car reverberates with raucous laughter as Roger recalls sitting in a meeting with the development agency, accepting their promises of support for the West Highland Free Press, then giving them a good old fashioned media kicking in a news story about other matters. He's an entertaining raconteur. "We never put a by-line on the news stories," he splutters. "I've always thought it a bad idea!"

Roger wrote a column once that described lunch with the then Chairman, Jim Hunter, in the Mustard Seed restaurant in Inverness. The restaurant has an upper level overlooking the river and Roger had a sudden vision of the HIE executive quaffing champagne while the masses scurried past on the pavement below. He used the tongue-in-cheek vision as the opening of his article. Hunter phoned him when it appeared. "Great piece," he told Roger, "but you realise people will believe it?" And they did, laughs Roger. To add insult to injury, Hunter was paying for lunch with his own money.

But the West Highland Free Press, would not have survived without HIDB, he admits. "In the late 1980s, HIDB identified that we were printing in Inverness and gave us a Heidelberg printing machine. It's the most dependable printing machine in the world. It never broke down. They did their homework and it wasn't cheap." It was the saviour of the Free Press. Roger smiles. He is not unaware of the irony.

In the mid-1970s Roger met the man who would bring him to work on the Isle of Skye. At the time, he was working in London, editing Time Out magazine. As a sports fanatic, he played football regularly. One night, a new player joined the game. He was vocal, argumentative, challenged constantly. Who the hell is he? Roger wondered. The answer was Brian Wilson, founder of the West Highland Free Press and future politician. Brian, who was born in Dunoon, whose mother was a Gaelic speaker from Islay and whose father was from Appin, went on to become a Labour politician, serving as a minister in the Scottish Office, the Department for Trade and Industry and the Foreign Office.

Raasay ferry

Roger Hutchinson, West Highland Free Press

The two men got on and Wilson would stay with Roger when he visited London. Did Roger fancy coming to work in Skye? Why not? He was bored with his job. He'd give Skye a year, he decided. It was November 1977 when he moved into the Gaelic speaking, crofting village of Drumfearn. "I got into the house and found I couldn't get TV reception. I switched on the radio and the only station I could receive was RTE in Dublin. I thought, this is so weird it's exactly right. It was like visiting another country without needing a passport."

As an Englishman, he has never encountered any anti-English sentiment on the island. Perhaps that's partly to do with the way Roger has chosen to integrate into his environment. "I could never bear, and still can't, people who move to the Gaidhealtachd and promptly claim to be Skye people. I'm just a writer and journalist from the north of England who is lucky enough to live here. My identity is no problem to me. I know who I am and always have."

When HIDB was first established, the major problems facing the Highlands and Islands were depopulation and unemployment. Now, the population is growing at 7.5% compared to 4.6% in the rest of Scotland. Employment stands at 78.2% as opposed to 72.4% in the rest of the country, although wages are also 10% lower. Roger Hutchinson is representative of a new wave of people who have moved into the area from other places in the last 50 years. But what has kept him here?

"It can be physically the most beautiful area of Europe. The whole area is spectacular. You never tire of it. But it is the people who have kept me here:

their sense of humour, their fortitude, their self-sufficiency, their adaptability, their hospitality, their generosity of spirit."

There is, he acknowledges, a distinctive culture. He may be a football fanatic but he had never heard of shinty until he arrived on Skye. As for the Gaelic language, he wishes he had learnt it years ago. You can't stay here without picking up a smattering but he would like to have learned it properly. Now, he says, there is a resurgence of interest in Gaelic, partly thanks to the Gaelic college at Sleat, Sabhal Mòr Ostaig, which has been hugely influential.

Isn't it a dying language? There are those in Scotland's central belt who might argue that it's public money being placed on a horse that's bound to fall at a hurdle eventually. "It's not a dying language; it's a minority language," argues Roger. There's a difference. It is, he says, worth supporting. "When any language dies, you become poorer for it. It's not just words that you lose. It's not just that the Eskimos have 50 words for snow and the Gaels have 50 words for rain. It's the means of seeing the world, or expressing a view of the world, that you lose."

Having an incoming population is vital in fragile areas. "The thing you have to remember is that culture is not part of DNA. You can be born in London and be put through Gaelic medium education and you'll be a little Sgitheanach like all the rest. It doesn't matter who your parents are."

HIDB and HIE's backing for Sabhal Mòr Ostaig was completely justified, he says. It has transformed Sleat economically, formerly one of the poorest areas on the island, and doubled its population. But he doesn't want them to be complacent. Skye has done well. So has the Inner Moray Firth which has become one of the most prosperous areas not just in the Highlands but in Scotland. Job done and congratulations, says Roger. But the story is different in some of the outlying areas.

Back at Sconser, I drive down to the car park at the ferry slipway. The boat that will take Roger back to Raasay is across on the island. Raasay, a jewel that is just 14 miles by 3, is an important part of HIDB's history. In the 1960s, the laird's

Portree in the morning light

house and other land were bought by Dr John Green. Green lived in Sussex and was nicknamed Dr No because of his resistance to any schemes that would raise employment or develop community assets. HIDB compulsorily purchased the property in 1979 and developed it, helping to secure the island's future.

It was the early stages of a community ownership policy that would come to mark HIE's progressive stance on land management. HIE didn't just have economic powers. It had far reaching social powers too and the development agency understood the importance of investing in village halls as well as factories. Their understanding of the importance of strengthening communities was at the heart of the agency's strategy and would guide them to ultimately back community land ownership schemes all over the Highlands and Islands.

Roger loves his house on Raasay overlooking the sea. The spirit of these islands drew him in and somehow a year turned into a lifetime. He is still a publicly spirited critic of the way public money is being spent in the Highland and Islands, but he recognises the extraordinary work that has been done across the area by HIE. "If HIDB had not been established, I don't like to think what would have happened to this entire region."

Just outside Broadford, the road curves and the sign for Skye's Gaelic college points right, leading across to the peninsula of Sleat. Sabhal Mòr Ostaig: the old barn of Ostaig. The original steading that lent its name to the Gaelic college stands further up the road from the main campus, nestling in a courtyard. Lovely old stone. Fine arched windows. The listed building dates back to the 1860s but is soon to open as an all year round conference centre. Back in the early 1970s, it was an old tumbledown ruin on a piece of land at Sleat, the seat of the Clan MacDonald, which had just been bought by Sir Iain Noble, a wealthy merchant banker.

Top: Sabhal Mòr Ostaig
Bottom: Donnie Munro, Director of Development, Sabhal Mòr Ostáig

The team and I put a lot of effort into supporting Gaelic which I firmly believe helped confidence levels around the Western Isles. I can remember people used to look down on Gaelic speakers. They thought it was an archaic language. Those who spoke it didn't want to shout it from the rooftops. I believe giving some investment to Gaelic, supporting Sabhal Mòr Ostaig, supporting the whole process of speaking Gaelic, helped significantly to increase confidence levels.

Sir Fraser Morrison,
HIE Chairman, 1992-1998

Sir Iain had bought 20,000 acres of the MacDonald estate which was being broken up to pay death duties. By chance, some old deeds had been thrown in. Without knowing it, he bought the old steading. He talked to friends about what he might do with the building and revealed a dream of turning it into a Gaelic college. Without Noble's vision and tenacity, there would be no college. It has grown organically in the 43 years since that conversation."

A dream grew into a scheme that grew into a grand plan. The college became not just a local specialist college, but a national centre for Gaelic – and an economic driver. "Iain Noble was a learner of the language," explains Donnie Munro, former lead singer with Runrig and now Director of Development for Sabhal Mòr Ostaig, "and someone who wanted to see a revival of the language aligned to economic development in the area. It was a pretty visionary step and probably seen as a pretty eccentric step too. But now, all of the parties within the Scottish Parliament recognise the value of the language at lots of different levels. The economic benefits of regenerating a language and a culture were understood."

Sleat, the 'garden of Skye' was one of the most socially deprived areas of the island but is now thriving economically and its population has doubled in size since the college opened. Sabhal Mòr Ostaig is the third biggest employer on Skye after the council and the NHS. The campus will be the site of the Kilbeg development, the first new village on Skye for 100 years, which will enable the college to expand its operation, with increased teaching and accommodation space. But Kilbeg will also offer local housing, a hotel, a residential care home, new enterprise units for businesses, and community leisure facilities.

The significance of Sabhal Mòr Ostaig has reached far beyond Skye. It has led a national conversation about the Gaelic language, spearheading a resurgence in awareness, confidence and interest and encouraging the growth of Gaelic medium education across Scotland. Four degrees are offered here in the Gaelic language including media studies, a course which feeds graduates to BBC Alba, and traditional music. The college, which has 70 full-time students and 300 distance learning students from around the world, rents out studio space to film Gaelic television series such as Bannan, and has a turnover of £5 million a year.

The college has truly become a centre for the community, with an on-site Gaelic medium nursery that is available to the public, and classes in a variety of leisure activities. Traditional Gaelic arts and culture have been emphasised. "Over time, the focus has shifted from the language itself to the wider context of the language," says Donnie Munro. "The centre can't exist in a vacuum. It's very important that the arts and the wider cultural heritage play an informing role in educational life."

The key, continues Donnie, is sustainability. "One of the things that became apparent was that the learning community were hugely important for the survival of the language and we couldn't rely on a diminishing number of native speakers which, after so many years of neglect, was at a very low ebb. We had to depend on a growing, vibrant community."

Light streams into Sabhal Mòr Ostaig, with floor to ceiling windows that look out across the water to Knoydart. It's an attractive space and the building also offers office accommodation to other local businesses, including Cànan, a web graphic design business that has an emphasis on Gaelic projects. Cànan's Operations Manager, Vanessa Lopez, is originally from Madrid but is one of the many incomers to the Highlands and Islands who have moved to the area as a result of increased jobs and housing opportunities. Vanessa has been on Skye for 12 years and now lives there with her partner and children.

"I saw an advert in the paper and thought it was a joke. I didn't think you would get a graphic design job on Skye. People don't realise the different lifestyles here. It's not just crofting and living off the land."

You have to adjust to an island when you are used to city life. "Life on Skye is different," says Vanessa. "It makes you think in a different way. It's two hours to get to a big supermarket but the safety is wonderful. My kids are wee and they run free and wild. It's the nature of living on an island."

Free and wild… yet convenient and accessible. It's the tightrope of economic development in the Highlands and Islands: retaining the magic while strengthening the possibilities of living and working here. The Scottish islands have the pull of the ancient and the push of the modern. On the one hand, you will pass islanders cutting peat from the earth as they have done for generations; on the other, you will see them checking iPhones. Driving from the college back to the Skye Bridge, the old barn of Ostaig seems to represent something: an amalgam of past and present and future. A future that retains some of the spirit of the old island that the poet Alexander Nicolson, who was writing at the time the steading was built, described.

'Many a poor black cottage is there,
Grimy with peat smoke,
Sending up in the soft evening air
Purest blue incense,
While the low music of psalm and prayer
Rises to Heaven.'

Alexander Nicolson

Venessa Lopez,
Operations Manager, Cànan

Strathpeffer to Glencoe

Outside the picturesque spa town of Strathpeffer, Ross-shire, the road to Dingwall offers a brief detour, climbing high up into the hills to the Heights of Brae before re-joining the main road. Up here, the panoramic view rolls gloriously and endlessly: to the left, the town of Dingwall sits in the jaws of the Moray Firth; to the right, Strathpeffer nestles in the sheltered safety of a valley. The summer day is warm and bright but in the distance, gulleys of snow still run on the high mountain tops like wrinkles on the face of the range.

At the heights, there is a monument to the early 20th century Highland writer Neil M. Gunn, author of 'The Silver Darlings'. There is nobody else here. The hilltop is mine; the silence broken only by the whisper of a gentle wind and the occasional bleat of sheep. The granite of the monument sparkles in the sunlight.

Gunn was born in Dunbeath but lived near Strathpeffer for 12 years, spending his afternoons walking in these hills after his morning writing session.

He wrote 11 of his 20 novels here, his work exploring the Highland communities and ways of life that he valued so highly. He wrote of the Clearances, the transition from one Highland way of life on the land to an enforced new way of life on the sea. And maybe that's the way it still is in the Highlands, a constant evolution to what is sustainable, to whatever can make this remote, geographically challenging, and beautiful area both economically and socially viable.

On the far hill, the turbines of a small wind farm turn rhythmically in the wind. Green energy taps into something that is both a challenge and an asset all over the Highlands and Islands: the wildness of the weather. The turbulence of the sea in the Pentland Firth, the ferocity of offshore and onshore wind. The elements cannot be tamed but they can certainly be harnessed and this is one of the most technologically advanced regions in the world in its attempts to do so.

Strathpeffer

Only a few miles separate the village of Strathpeffer from Dingwall. It's a one-street town, grey stone with an absence of gloss. But it has character, this place, and pride. On a Saturday, the navy, white and red scarves peep from jackets as the fans flow down to the Global Energy stadium where local team Ross County play. The town has just over 5,000 inhabitants but at times the stadium sees crowds of 6,000 at matches, the team supported from around the whole county.

"You can't be a real country," rock star Frank Zappa once said, "unless you have a beer and an airline. It helps if you have some kind of football team or some nuclear weapons but at the very least you need a beer." On that score, the county of Ross-shire is half way to being a country. In a beautiful pastoral area that is rich in farmland, the niche Black Isle Brewery started out producing organic beer in a shed and now exports across

Europe and Asia, from Stockholm to Tokyo. The Highlands and Islands are full of enterprises that should, by rights, be small but punch well above their weight because of big hearts and big ambitions. No better example than Ross County. The team has gone from the Scottish third division to become the most northerly Premier League club in Scotland.

Strathpeffer   Tore   Dingwall   Loch Ness   Drumnadrochit   Fort Augustus   Spean Bridge   Lochailort

I think that quiet confidence is a very attractive part of what we have and what we are about. I don't want us to become over expressive about how confident we are. But lack of confidence and a negative frame of mind is not a good way to be. I don't think Scottish reserve is an obstacle to success. I think it's a strength.

Sir Fraser Morrison,
HIE Chairman 1992-1998

Driving into the grounds of Ross County, it's impossible not to be impressed by the facilities. The club is under the leadership of Roy MacGregor, chairman of Global Energy Group, and has the reputation for being forward thinking and progressive. The Highland Football Academy is sited here, the plaques on the wall acknowledging funding from HIE, Highland Council and Europe. The plaques are a familiar sight all over the Highlands and Islands, testimony to what might never have been without collaboration and investment. The Youth Academy is a superb training facility for young players from all over the area and offers gym and training facilities for Ross County players that are second to none.

A small, compact figure in jeans bustles into reception and smiles. Steven Ferguson is a former captain of Ross County and is now head of youth and development here. He manages an under-9s and under-17s team and exudes the kind of energy and commitment necessary to carry such a challenging post over a vast area. His young players need that dedication too. "The area we have to cover is the size of Belgium and you can be in Fort William one day and Skye the next. Kids can travel three hours from Orkney to here, then travel for four hours to play for the youth team. That's the commitment we've got."

Farmers' Market, Dingwall

Steven was a terrier of a player in his time, the kind who hassled and harried and drove his team forward. He left the club back in 2003 for Ayr United but returned in a coaching role in 2010. He and his wife had fallen in love with the area first time round. "It was away from the rat race," he says. They had no hesitation in returning.

Things were different when he left. "When I was here first, we were in the third division and it was beyond our wildest dreams to get to the Premier League." Inverness Caledonian Thistle is around 15 miles away, and having two Premier League football clubs has helped give a sporting status to the Highlands. "It's massive for the area," says Steven. "The number of people coming to the Highlands for football is huge – people who had never been to Dingwall before."

Outside, bright sunshine streams onto the empty pitch as we stand in the deserted stadium. Even when empty it has a special quality, encased on all four sides so that it feel cocooned, suspended from the rest of the world. On match days, the sound is trapped in here, reverberating round the stadium and creating an electricity that players from all over Scotland appreciate. "It's one of the best stadium facilities in the country. There are no complaints from anyone who plays here. It's a unique place to play and watch football. There's been lots of investment by Roy MacGregor and what he's done here is looked on fondly by the rest of Scottish football who appreciate the position he's got the club in."

The club is relatively new to the Scottish Premier League, joining after victory in the first division in the 2011-12 season. But it has a long history, dating back to 1929 when it was part of the Highland League. The club badge has a Caberfeidh, or stag's head, which is taken from the badge of the Seaforth Highlanders, the regiment that many Ross-shire locals had fought and died in during the First World War. As a result, Ross County are known as "The Staggies".

In 2010, Ross County beat Celtic to take their place in the Scottish Cup final. "We took 28,000 supporters to the final and it was a real family occasion," says Steven. "Historically, we're very much part of the community."

Steven Ferguson, Head of Youth and Community, Ross County F.C.

Ross County were beaten by Dundee United but it didn't dampen their ambition. "We're a team from Dingwall – but we don't need to think like a team from Dingwall."

Above the entrance to the club is a strapline. 'More than just a football club,' it says. That commitment is taken seriously. The club has charitable status and is involved in a number of community initiatives, including a scheme that uses football memories to help people with Alzheimer's and a scheme designed to remove the stigma from mental illness. "We're serving our community not just in football," explains Steven.

There's a good feeling at Ross County. Open. Warm. Innovative. There's also a clear sense of identity. "We know who we are. We know we're mixing with the big boys and we can take a couple of minutes to say we're punching above our weight here but that's why we are effective. We want to be the best we can be. We know that a town of this size shouldn't be in the Premier League – but we are."

There's also a good balance at Ross County: a have-a-go attitude combined with enough humility to be grounded. You get the impression that even if the Barcelona team turned up in Dingwall, Ross County would try to play like they could win. Positive Mental Attitude. Scottish football manager John Lambie knows all about that. He was once told while watching a match that one of his players, who had been taken off injured, was concussed and didn't know who he was. "That's great," said Lambie. "Tell him he's Pele and get him back on."

I always think there's a correlation between confidence and sporting success.

Sandy Cumming,
HIE Chief Executive, 2000-2010

Ross County v Inverness Caledonian Thistle at Victoria Park, Dingwall

Dingwall to Tore and onto Inverness. From there, the road to Fort William winds down the side of Loch Ness, past the picturesque tourist village of Drumnadrochit with its Nessie exhibition and boat rides, and on to Fort Augustus, where the 60-mile long Caledonian Canal bisects the village. Eight miles from Fort William, the inspiring bronze figures of the Commando memorial at Spean Bridge appear on the horizon, the three men looking down from a height over the spectacular valley of the River Spean, with the peaks of Ben Nevis and Aonach Mòr visible in the distance. One of the most iconic and famous war memorials in Scotland, it is a tribute to the British Commandos and overlooks the old commando training depot that was established at Achnacarry Castle in 1942.

Designed by the late Wick-born sculptor Scott Sutherland, who won a national competition to get the commission, the striking memorial tells a story not just of the war effort but of the commandos who trained all over Lochaber. In a modern industrial estate on the outskirts of Fort William, the Headquarters of Marine Harvest is less striking, more functional, but tells an important Highland story too. It is the story of Scottish fish farming, an industry that was born in the 1960s and developed into a key component of the Highlands and Islands economy.

"HIDB played a key part in the development of the industry," says Steve Bracken, Business Support Manager of Marine Harvest. "There's no doubt about it."

Fish farming was not universally popular. There was a lot of opposition from people who didn't want to see a fish cage in the loch. You do have to accept change, though. If you want to see thriving schools in our more remote areas, you have to accept these industries coming in.

Sandy Cumming,
HIE Chief Executive, 2000-2010

Steve had a degree in geography and was working as a porter at Edinburgh Royal Infirmary when he saw a job advert in the Oban Times for a vacancy at a fish farm run by Unilever. He didn't know what was involved but it sounded interesting. He wanted a job in the outdoors and a fish farm offered that. In May 1977, he was taken on as a supervisor at Scotland's first fish farm at Lochailort. "I was responsible for a small team and on day one I was told, 'Here's a boat.' It was challenging! But anybody could have been a fish farm supervisor in those days. There were no rule books. Today I wouldn't get a foot in the door it's so technical."

Loch Ness, Invermoriston

Commando Memorial,
Spean Bridge in the Great Glen

*People ask specially for Scottish salmon
in the shops. It's a strong industry
for the Highlands and Islands.
Local people have developed small
smokehouses all over the area, from
Applecross to Shieldaig to Argyll.
Some also smoke cheese. One in
Lochaber even smoked alligator…*

Iain Robertson,
HIE Chief Executive, 1991-2000

He learned on the job and has now been with the company, which has changed ownership a number of times, for 38 years. "We started with trout but quickly realised salmon was more profitable," he recalls. Back in 1971, Scotland produced 14 tonnes of salmon. Today, it is 160,000 tonnes, of which Marine Harvest, part of the biggest fish processing company in the world, produces 48,000. Salmon is the largest food export from Scotland (and the UK), and combined with whisky, accounts for 90% of Scotland's total food and drink exports.

In the early days of fish farming, Marine Harvest wanted to rent loch space from The Crown Estate and to find a willing landlord so started discussion with Mrs Pauline Cameron-Head, a colourful character who owned Inverailort Castle. The area was perfect, with good access to both fresh and sea water

plus some flat land nearby that had outbuildings left from the war. "Mrs Cameron-Head loved the idea of jobs being created in the Highlands," recalls Steve. "Lochailort had been a training camp during the war and there were a lot of old commando buildings. She agreed to rent out the land and buildings."

Lochailort is one of the most sheltered lochs in Scotland, surrounded on all sides by hills. Unilever had begun a research operation there in 1965, developing fish farming methods, but this was their first farm and the equipment used was still basic. It was a new industry with a steep learning curve ahead but the potential for the Highlands was obvious from the start. "There were a lot of discussions with HIDB who played a big part and were extremely supportive," recalls Steve.

Unilever developed a technique that involved moving the fish from freshwater to seawater and patented it. But it wasn't exactly rocket science. HIDB paid just a pound for the patent with a view to encouraging and developing fish farming across other parts of the Highlands and Islands.

Originally, HIDB thought that the industry would be an ideal addition to crofting. "The idea was that you could have a few pens of fish at the loch end of a croft but the great vision didn't come about. Any animal can suffer disease. Sea lice started to appear and it was a big challenge for fish farmers," says Steve. Infection control was vital and fish farming needed professional, specialist back-up, not a part-time amateur approach. It became evident that major investment was needed in good pens and nets. "Success in salmon farming is all about scale."

UCI Mountain Bike World Cup, Fort William

Unilever expanded abroad, even sending a small team from Fort William to Chile to establish fish farms there. For Steve, the fish farming journey would take him to Sri Lanka for two-and-a-half years to iron out difficulties the company was having with tiger prawn farms. "It was fascinating, so different from salmon. Everything was different… culturally, climatically, environmentally." Did it take him long to settle? He grins. "About 20 minutes. I loved it. I would have stayed longer."

He was based in a small town north of Colombo but it took no time to reach the countryside. It was hill country, full of tea plantations, many of which were named after Scotland. Edinburgh, Glasgow, Balmoral… Steve looked at the landscape and thought of home. "Not Glencoe but maybe the Ochils." He came home from the sunshine of Sri Lanka on a Friday and on the Monday morning was sent to Shetland in horizontal rain. But while he would have happily stayed longer abroad, he didn't mind being home really. Lochaber has so many attractions. Good schools, hillwalking, cycling… the great outdoors.

It's the pattern for many who live in the Highlands and Islands. Their work may take them away at some stage, but the area's magic lures them back eventually. Then their children go through the same process. Steve's daughter works as an actress in London but loves coming home. His son is a sculptor and artist in the Highlands, and part of a project that gets schoolchildren involved in art. He insists on being based in the Highlands but also works abroad for spells.

The business years between 1971 and 1992 were unpredictable for fish farming, with good spells and bad. By 1992, Unilever had invested a great deal in the business and been involved in pioneering research and development. Around this time the decision was taken by Unilever to focus on fast-moving consumer goods, meaning that its operations in agribusiness no longer fitted with the company vision.

Marine Harvest's feed trial unit at Lochailort

Steve Bracken, Business Support Manager, Marine Harvest

Unilever decided to sell. A succession of owners took over for brief periods but the company is now owned by a Norwegian company and run from Bergen. It doesn't matter, says Steve, that the company is under foreign ownership. Scottish whisky companies, after all, have French, Italian and Canadian owners. "The important thing is that the owner understands the business and is prepared to invest."

Marine Harvest have been prepared to invest. They have also continued Unilever's policy of wanting to work in partnership with landowners and communities. Proposals for new fish farms have been put to different Highlands and Islands communities but the communities' decisions have been accepted. A proposed farm on the island of Canna would have given six full-time jobs. The 15-strong community was split eight to seven against and the company moved on to Muck, which has a population of 32. "They were very supportive. We have built three houses on the island and set up a community trust fund that we put money into each year for local causes."

The island of Colonsay, population 120, has welcomed Marine Harvest's proposal of a new farm and the company has built a new £20 million hatchery at Lochailort and has another £20 million plan for Glenmoriston. It is important for infection control that farms are not placed too close together, explains Steve, but that has benefits for small communities. "The great thing about salmon farming is it provides jobs in remote, rural areas."

The fish from the different farms across the Highlands and Islands are taken to be processed at a separate plant in Fort William where they are gutted, cleaned and boxed. Everything else is based here at HQ, including the company's managing director; the environmental and health teams; company vets; occupational health and human resources. In the foyer outside Steve's office, the history of Marine Harvest is charted right across the wall from 1965 onwards.

Strathpeffer   Tore   Dingwall   Loch Ness   Drumnadrochit   Fort Augustus   Spean Bridge   Lochailort

Highlights include being granted the Royal Warrant in 1990 to supply fresh salmon to the Queen, and the achievement of the Label Rouge Accreditation in 1992, the first food item outside of France to be given the honour. "It's great," says Steve, "to be part of a business with so much potential."

Fort William is dubbed the Outdoor Capital of the UK with good reason. Walking, climbing, skiing, and snowboarding. Fishing, sailing, kayaking and mountain biking. It's all here in a natural playground that is set in an area of stunning natural beauty.

Scotland has a number of ski ranges: the Cairngorms, Glenshee, Nevis Range and the Lecht. But just a short drive from Fort William is the country's oldest resort, established almost 60 years ago in Glencoe. In a good year, the ski season can last here from December to May, but the resort has additional dry slope facilities. Glencoe is also part of the famous West Highland Way, a 96-mile route that runs from Glasgow to Fort William and is used by 85,000 walkers each year.

Investment from HIE has led to 10 pods being built at the ski resort, mini lodges made of wood and natural materials which are promoted as "glamorous camping". The pods are tiny with just enough room for four berths but with some of the perks of a cottage: kettle, fridge, television, and microwave.

The plateau at the Glencoe Mountain Resort

Glencoe is more than a resort. It would be hard to find somewhere more atmospheric than this place which was the site of the famous 1692 massacre of 38 members of the Clan MacDonald. Months before the massacre, King William had offered Highland clans a pardon for their part in the Jacobite uprising as long as they swore an oath of allegiance to him before a set date. The chief of Glencoe arrived at Fort William to take the oath but was told he had to travel another 70 miles to Inverary. He missed the date by days but was assured his oath was accepted; his people were safe.

The next month 120 troops arrived at Glencoe under the command of Captain Robert Campbell of Glenlyon. The Clan MacDonald offered them Highland hospitality: food, drink and lodgings. Ten days later, the massacre began with the visitors turning on the hosts, houses being burned and MacDonald fleeing the scene. The clan had been victims of what was called "murder under trust" which was considered worse than ordinary murder under Scots law. It came to be seen as not just an act of aggression but of a betrayal of decency.

Something of those events remains here. Simultaneously bleak and beautiful, imposing and melancholy, the road forces its way through the mountains, rising and falling, twisting and turning. Time is a theme you return to repeatedly when journeying through the Highlands and Islands. Yes, there is progress and development. There is initiative, imagination, entrepreneurship. But in so much of this area, there is a strong sense of the enduring, of a landscape that has absorbed history quietly, breathes it, reflects it, but remains essentially impervious to change because of man's inability to tame it.

Back in 1889, Black's picturesque Tourist Guide described part of the stage coach route from Ballachulish Pier to Glencoe:

'The road enters the neck of Glencoe at the Bridge of Coe, skirting the river between two huge mountains, some green patches and ruined huts by the river side indicating the place where the massacre occurred. The cluster of precipitous mountains whose rugged summits impart such wildness to this scene has been aptly called the Alps of Glencoe. A crowd of mountains, heaped in wild confusion, stamped by sublimity and grandeur.'

Over a century later, the feeling in this glen is the same. Events seem stamped on the landscape. Darkness and light, and a sense that centuries may go by, and progress may be made, but some things are absorbed in memory simply because their essential truth should never be forgotten.

Late afternoon light on River Coe and the Three Sisters in Glen Coe

… *The road winds in*
Listlessness of ancient war,
Langour of broken steel
Clamour of confused wrong, apt
In silence. Memory is strong
Beyond the bone,

Rannoch by Glencoe, TS Eliot

Campbeltown to **Brodick**

There's a tendency to see HIDB and HIE as bodies that gave grants and built factories. That's important but it's much more complicated than that. The key to this is self-confidence.

Jim Hunter,
HIE Chairman, 1998-2004

Summer night has fallen in Campbeltown. Through my window in the Royal Hotel, garlands of fairy lights shimmer blue in the darkness, lighting the path of the esplanade, outlining the drooping arch of the palm trees. The water in the harbour is like inky glass. Green and red lights glow on the pier, guiding in a small boat that glides through the still waters, its reflection visible on the polished surface.

The room within is comfortable and stylish. Tasteful furnishings with just a hint of tartan in a muted check on the bed runner; a spacious, high gloss bathroom. Downstairs, the hotel restaurant has had a busy evening, serving dinner to both residents and passing trade. Yet, just a short time ago this building was derelict, rundown and barricaded, a symbol of a dying community and troubling economic conditions. A crumbling townhouse. A cinema in need of renovation. An empty Jaeger factory that at its height employed 180 people to produce high quality men's suits but which eventually couldn't compete with alternative low cost production elsewhere. In the worst times, the percentage of unemployed people hit double figures and was well above the Scottish average. Campbeltown was on its uppers.

All day here, people have been talking about the ship that was spotted in the upgraded harbour yesterday. A massive tanker, apparently. Far bigger than the usual ships that carry the wind turbines out of the local factory, Wind Towers Scotland, which employs around 130 people. It's being viewed as an optimistic sign, all the comings and goings in the new harbour. This is an industrial town and a lot goes out by sea rather than road because of its remote location. Movement in the harbour is a sign of a new wind blowing.

Fifty million pounds of public and private money has been ploughed into Campbeltown and it has brought with it a surge of optimism. An investment of £5.2 million has been made into a new social housing development;

£2.8 million on redeveloping the local cinema; £22 million on creating the Machrihanish Dunes resort. The resort includes both the Royal and Ugadale hotels, timeshare cottages, a pub, and a new links golf course at Machrihanish Dunes. The old Jaeger factory has now been developed into six business units. Then there's the harbour renovation; a leisure centre; and the money given to local businesses to smarten up their shop frontages. The economic interventions have brought the local unemployment rate down to 2.3%.

Five years ago, Campbeltown looked and felt very different. "The town went through a bad patch but there's a whole new vibe," says Graeme McMurchy of Campbeltown Motor Company. "The older, dilapidated buildings have been knocked down. There wasn't much industry left but it's really turned a corner. Born and raised here, Graeme says the town is notable for its community spirit. Fundraising efforts always achieve more than their targets and now that there has been public investment, people are feeling energised. "It's like anything in life," he says. "Money invested lifts you."

Campbeltown Harbour

It's a smell from the forbidden playgrounds of a city childhood: the nostalgic scent of old ruined houses, of damp walls and crumbling plaster. Today it fills The Picture House in Campbeltown – but here it's about regeneration, not dilapidation. Renovation work has begun on the A-listed building, with ripped out cinema seats piled in a heap in the auditorium which was designed by the renowned cinema architect Albert Victor Gardner and opened in 1913.

It's a quirky, unusual cinema. High up, on either side of the stage which houses the screen, are two decorative "wee houses" as they are known locally. "The design was intended to create the illusion of an outdoor scene," explains retired teacher Sid Gallagher, an Irishman who has lived in Campbeltown since the 1980s and is part of a local committee organising the restoration of the historic building. "Like a Spanish street scene with the ceiling being the blue sky. We will be restoring its 1930s look but with modern materials and low energy running costs, with LED lights instead of gas, and more comfortable seats."

It is not only land that communities in Scotland can now gain assistance to buy, but buildings, renewable energy schemes… anything that can be turned into a public asset. The Picture House is the oldest continuously run, purpose-built cinema in Scotland still showing films, and this new lease of life will secure its future. The building will be leased to a cinema operator who will run it for the community seven days a week and the money for rental will be used for any continuing maintenance.

The building re-opens in 2016 and not only will it operate as a cinema, the stage will be used for theatre shows, music and events, and the building will also house conferences. Live events from places like Covent Garden can even be streamed here and before the restoration work began, the Picture House's committee had experimented by showing a live stream from America of Orlando Bloom performing in Shakespeare's Romeo and Juliet. "It will be a cultural hub," says Sid. "It gives you a beautiful building in the middle of town and people coming in on the ferry will see it instantly."

Is there enough demand in a small town to make its 240 seats viable? Sid believes there is. A travelling production of Whisky Galore by the Mull Theatre Company, which toured all over the Highlands, had more ticket sales in Campbeltown than anywhere else apart from Inverness's theatre, Eden Court. "It's a real example of community

The Picture House, Campbeltown currently undergoing restoration

spirit in Campbeltown." There has been a concerted effort to bring pride back to the historic town centre and conservation area and people feel it's working. "The centre of town is covered in scaffolding but it's a good feeling to know it's being done up," says Sid.

Round the corner, in the town's main shopping area, the pungent smell of fish drifts onto the street. There are the usual displays of fresh sea food in Archie Macmillan's shop window but also a selection of home-made produce. Fish cakes. Salmon quiche. And it looks like multi-culturalism has reached Campbeltown in the form of roasted salmon pakora.

Archie is a character, wild grey hair and a fisherman's jumper with the sleeves rolled up, an open, friendly handshake that is accompanied by a look that holds a healthy hint of suspicion for strangers.

You can tell he's a grafter with plenty of energy. "People don't want to work so hard these days," he complains. Hard work has brought him success. He is in talks with Fortnum and Mason in London and hopes by the end of the year to be supplying the exclusive store with Scottish smoked haddock and sides of salmon. He also supplies Epic foods in Singapore with salmon, cheese and mussels.

Originally from the fishing village of Carradale, 16 miles from Campbeltown, he owned his own fishing boat by the time he was 23. But fishing declined and boats dwindled and in the end there was no herring and no money. Archie began fishing for scallops all year round and even exported them but eventually he needed a change of direction. He bought a shop and smokehouse in Campbeltown from owner Donnie Gilchrist. "He was 76

at the time," recalls Archie. "He said he'd stay two or three weeks to show me the ropes. He stayed 12 years."

Working until he was 88? They're made of stern stuff in Kintyre. Archie has made his business work even when economic times were tough – but those who diversify usually thrive. Would he have had even more success in a bigger place with more opportunity? "It's fine here," he says with the kind of understatement that denotes sincerity. "I've had a better life here than in the city. You don't need as much money. And the fresh air means you live longer."

The scaffolding that Sid talked about earlier is evident when I walk round the town. But as the day wears on, it becomes apparent that the real support structures of Campbeltown are its people. It is their energy, pride and commitment that have become the building bricks of regeneration.

Getting digital connectivity is a game changer. It's a top priority. Most of the region wouldn't have seen fibre optic broadband commercially, but we've stepped in and now over 80% of homes and businesses will have good quality, high speed solutions by the end of 2016. I don't want any part of the Highlands and Islands to be without a potential solution. We'll get there – but not everybody can be first.

Alex Paterson,
HIE Chief Executive, 2010 to present

"Unattended children will be given an espresso and a puppy," says the notice on the wall of the entrance to the restaurant in the Ugadale Hotel. It's a typical shot of humour from a hotel whose visitor book glows with tributes about customer service. In a window seat in the restaurant overlooking the spectacular Machrihanish Dunes, is general manager Kevin Lewis, a big American from Arizona with a tongue-in-cheek nature. The Machrihanish Dunes Resort is owned by his employer, Boston based company Southworth Development.

Kevin, a trained golf pro, moved here with his wife in 2008 and spent three years managing the project until his visa ran out. Now back, there is something about the area that draws him. "I could camp here for the rest of my life," he admits. "It seemed like stepping back in time 30 or 40 years at first. Some of the attitudes and the way of life weren't quite as close to modern day as I was used to at home but I am a simple guy and don't require a lot of modern things. We found it quite relaxing, less hectic, less intense." 'Date night' with his wife, he says, involves going for a Chinese meal and a film in Campbeltown.

Machrihanish has a long history as a resort. The original Machrihanish golf course has views over Islay, Jura and the community owned island of Gigha, and dates back to the 1870s. It was formed with the help of the legendary golf pro and course designer Old Tom Morris and has one of the most famous opening holes in golf. This area was also once one of the whisky capitals of the world with 34 distilleries. But most closed and the whisky barons disappeared, and the resort lost its lustre. "Our goal," says Kevin, "is to turn this into the destination resort it's meant to be and was 100 years ago when this hotel was the place to go."

Southworth's involvement is an example of the kind of inward investment HIE are continually trying to encourage in remote areas like the Kintyre peninsula. "The company invested £20 million," explains Kevin, "and without HIE help, the prospect of success probably wouldn't have been as optimistic. It made a difference to whether we did it or not."

He and his wife left their daughter, a country singer in Nashville, to take the job in Scotland. "Thank goodness for Skype and text messaging," he says. Until recently, connectivity has been a challenge for parts of the Highlands and Islands. Kevin, like so many others in the area, has been eagerly awaiting the arrival of better broadband in Campbeltown, which became available in the summer of 2015.

The story of connectivity in the Highlands is a major part of the story of HIDB and HIE. The improvement of roads and transport, particularly the A9, has improved the accessibility of the Highlands from other parts of Scotland. But in the 1980s, the agency realised that digital connectivity was also vital to the region. They would have to embrace new technology quickly if they wanted to participate in the emerging computer based economy. The board approved a significant investment of £4.9 million to BT to ensure that 43 of the main areas of population within the Highlands and Islands were connected to the new Integrated Services Digital Network (ISDN).

It was the biggest single investment they had ever made. It was also a shrewd move that would see the Highlands and Islands strengthen its position in ways that similarly rural regions did not. It gave the region, normally seen as last in line, a head start on other places, ensuring they were not left behind in the emergence of this new digital age. The board's quick thinking turned out to be a major benefit to both existing businesses and new inward investors and further upgrades and investments were made using European Objective 1 funding.

Kevin Lewis,
Royal Hotel, Campbeltown

The Royal Hotel, Campbeltown

Campbeltown   Machrihanish   Tarbert   Portavadie   Loch Fyne   Claonaig   Lochranza   Brodick   River Spey

Around the same time, HIE started developing a number of office parks on the edges of towns in the hope of attracting new businesses. Several offices were built in Alness and the agency persuaded BT to move in. BT set up a helpdesk there for their own employees, helping them with their use of the emerging internet. Gradually, the Highlands and Islands gathered a growing number of businesses that wanted to establish contact centres in the region. Today these include TalkTalk, who operate from Stornoway, Webhelp in Rothesay and Dunoon, while Capita services contracts for household names from Forres. In addition some of the world's largest IT companies – Atos, Capgemini and Fujitsu – have provided hundreds of jobs in the area.

We quickly sussed out that if we were going to wait for ISDN to be installed, we were going to wait a long time. The Highlands always got things last. We worked out a deal with BT. The association started before the end of HIDB and was finalised during my time. We gave them something like £5 million to accelerate the rollout of ISDN. Because of that, we were able to take a couple of bold steps.

Iain Robertson,
HIE Chief Executive, 1991-2000

Superfast broadband launch in Evanton

For the first time, we could do things in the Highlands on phone lines. We weren't reliant on rail and road for that and we could maximise the opportunity of the internet – which wasn't called the internet then. It just played right into our hands.

Iain Robertson,
HIE Chief Executive, 1991-2000

Technology does not stand still. HIE has continued over the years to recognise the importance of digital connectivity to the region's ability to compete and it has become one of their top priorities.
In 1996, a deal was announced to improve mobile coverage in the area. Four million pounds was invested in a £46 million joint Vodaphone and Cellnet project to introduce 200 mobile masts across the region. The concept of mast sharing was introduced for the first time and the take-up of mobile technology both by businesses and the public exceeded all targets for the project.

In 2010, the region was one of four areas across the UK to be chosen to pilot a revolutionary broadband project and in 2013, HIE signed a new £146 million project with BT to ensure at least 84% of the Highlands and Islands will have access to superfast broadband services by 2016. The agency has also been given money by the Scottish Government to manage Community Broadband Scotland, not just in the region but across the country as a whole. This project will ensure that remote areas, like the 16% of the Highlands and Islands that won't have access to superfast broadband through the first phase of the BT contract, will have workable alternatives to bring internet technology to their homes and businesses.

For areas like Campbeltown, improvements can't come soon enough. Internet sales and marketing have become increasingly important for businesses and connectivity is vital for attracting inward investment. Long-term, Kevin's goal is to increase occupancy at the Machrihanish Dunes resort and to continue to look for other suitable investments for Southworth. "Campbeltown is a natural tourist place for yachts," he says, "and there is the potential for cruise ships. It's not exploited enough. Our goal is to help the community too. Helping them helps us."

Digital connectivity underpins everything. With broadband, we can get new models of working and attract additional inward investment.

Alex Paterson,
HIE Chief Executive, 2010 to present

There is something almost eerie about the old Machrihanish airbase that once housed around 1,000 military personnel. A lone security sentry sits isolated in a box at the gate of the vast expanse of flat ground. Accommodation blocks lie empty while outcrops of huts and outbuildings huddle together. An old church. A bowling alley. Silence blows through the base like a chill wind. The striking, flat expanse of ground is like a scene from an atmospheric movie but it's more than that. When the RAF withdrew from Machrihanish in the 1990s, the decision was viewed with dismay. Now the site is being described as 1,000 acres of opportunity.

Following a successful community buy-out it is now owned by Machrihanish Airbase Community Company (MACC), a social enterprise with weighty ambitions to turn it into a site that offers both social and economic benefits for the community. The site has around 50 tenants employing 170 people. An array of local clubs, with members young and old, use the facilities every week, and there is a calendar of events such as the MACC Challenge and the MACH1 Rally that appeal to both locals and those from further afield. It feels like those ambitions are well underway.

The office of Malcolm McMillan, the young Business Development Manager for MACC, is a strange place to work. From his window, the factory of Wind Towers (Scotland) Ltd, who rent space on the base, is visible but otherwise there is not much human

Malcolm McMillan of the Machrihanish Airbase Community Company

contact here. Or so you'd think. There are actually around 50 tenants here, but the site is so vast that the other tenants are largely out of sight.

Machrihanish had been occupied by the military since the 1940s. By 1995, the strategic importance of the site as a Cold War airfield had disappeared and it was put on care and maintenance before being handed back to the Ministry of Defence. They had no clear vision for development and in 2008 MACC was formed with a view to taking ownership of it. The site was finally handed over to the community in May 2012 and for many it was an opportunity to create local employment for young people.

"The closure of the airbase contributed to depopulation," explains Malcolm, who returned to the area against his own expectations after university. "The group's ambition was to open up the site for development and job creation. For local young people, opportunities are limited and many have to leave the area so the general vision is create jobs and bolster the local economy. There has been a lot of boom and bust over the years in Campbeltown and we are trying to avoid that in the business portfolio."

MACC already makes a profit. "The first business plan was to break even by year three but we have made a profit each year." The money is coming from rental of existing property and the longer

term strategy is to utilise as much of the site as possible to create employment and wider benefits for the community. "It's got Scotland's longest runway and 200 buildings… it doesn't lend itself to one use anymore." What is clear is the sheer diversity of business development happening on the site.

MACC is in discussion with a company regarding an onshore aquaculture project and both solar farms and biomass energy projects are being considered. But perhaps the most unusual and exciting opportunity is the possibility of Machrihanish becoming the UK's first spaceport. At the moment, the UK doesn't have a facility for launching satellites.

A number of areas have been chosen
as potential sites and to Malcolm's delight,
Machrihanish is one.

The interest is despite knowing that most
spaceports don't always make a great deal
of money. "Spaceport America only has
30-40 full-time personnel but the supply
chain is where the benefits are. That provides
3-4,000 jobs, while the construction of the
project spent over $212 million." A spaceport
would not only be a launch for satellites
but for space travel tourism, such as that
proposed by Virgin Galactic. "Nobody really
knows the answers because it's catering for
a market that doesn't yet exist."

*It hasn't just been about
spending money.
We tried to create long-term
engines of positive change.*

Willy Roe,
HIE Chairman, 2004-2012

For Malcolm it's a surprise to find himself here at his desk. He never expected to come back to the area after graduating from Edinburgh University. "Being away and seeing other parts of Scotland makes you realise what you are missing. Before, it was all I knew and it seemed boring."

He estimates that only about 20 of his school year of 100 are still in the area. He might not have thought he would be one but he's married and settled here now, can see the appeal of this place and this job in the middle of a deserted airbase. "Campbeltown has gone through a vast amount of change in the last six or seven years. There's a lot of work gone into rejuvenating it and it's very positive. It's a nice place to live."

The roads through Argyll are lined with rhododendrons in June, the lush blooms a vibrant magenta in places, in others a delicate baby pink. They burst through burgeoning green foliage and the landscape feels rich and heavy with growth, fuelled by sunshine and rain. All along the coast, CalMac boats are visible, choppy froth following in their wake, as they travel from one tip of Scotland to another, from port to port, from mainland to the network of small islands that litter the Argyll coast.

The reason the organisation has been a success is its ability to connect with local communities.

Sandy Cumming,
HIE Chief Executive, 2000-2010

As the road dips, the rain dries and the pretty port of Tarbert opens out, the water sparkling in sunshine. A short crossing on the ferry leads to Portavadie, where the hammering and sawing of construction fills the air. A new spa has been built, with a pool, gym and leisure complex that boasts spectacular views across Loch Fyne to the Island of Arran. This site was originally built as a dry dock for concrete oil rigs. By the time the place was finished in 1975, at a cost of £17 million, the industry had moved to steel rigs instead of concrete. Portavadie sat silent and sullen for 30 years, a white elephant in Scotland's sitting room that nobody wanted to mention. But in 2009 Portavadie opened as a marina. HIE has invested over £1 million in the development of this upmarket holiday resort with truly opulent surroundings and the marina at its heart. "HIE are enablers," says General Manager, Iain Jurgensen. "If they hadn't invested, we would be three to five years behind where we are." The resort is a long-term project to make Portavadie the world class spa hotel and holiday facility they want it to be. "This is a marathon not a sprint. Portavadie needs to get to the stage it can re-invest by itself."

Owned by the Scottish entrepreneurs the Bulloch family, it has a number of bars and restaurants, a children's playpark and a 9-hole golf course to encourage families to stay here. "We have world-class expectations," says Iain Jurgensen. "But our ambition is to become a destination that is inclusive, not exclusive. It's all about attracting people to come two hours off the beaten track."

Portavadie offers 85 jobs – a significant employer – in a beautiful but remote location. Around half the staff are locals, with the rest being brought in from outside, many from abroad. Jodie Bramall is a young graduate

who came to the west coast to work for a summer and stayed. "I love the west coast. I thought I'd end up here but maybe not at this stage. But I made a lot of friends, met my partner, and I'm a sucker for the scenery."

Iain Jurgensen became one of the youngest executive chefs of a 5-Star resort in Scotland at the age of 27, running a team of 60 at St Andrews. He has tried to surround himself with people of similar calibre and brought in Stephen McCafferty, whose track record includes the renowned Cameron House Hotel on Loch Lomond, to run the new spa facility. Stephen stays five days a week before returning home to his family in the Glasgow area at the weekend. "This is one of the top five spas in Britain," he says. "The location, the view the design… I feel like I'm going on holiday when I'm driving here. I love it."

Tourism is a key part of what the Highlands and Islands has to offer and is therefore an important sector for HIE to invest in. Ten miles from Tarbert is the hamlet of Claonaig where a summer ferry runs to Lochranza on the north of the Island of Arran in North Ayrshire. It's a short crossing to the picturesque village which has a castle complete with underground prison and from there, a 20-mile drive to the main town on the island, Brodick.

Nestling in extensive gardens at Brodick, just minutes from the ferry slipway where the boat crosses from Ardrossan all year round, is Scotland's hotel of the year. The exclusive Auchrannie resort which, with 160 jobs attached, is the biggest employer on the island apart from the NHS. It's a beautiful hotel with a spa, pool, bars and restaurants and also a number of self-catering properties in the grounds, the kind of luxury tourist attraction that would once have been unthinkable on Arran.

Top: Portavadie Marina
Bottom: The Auchrannie Resort on Arran

Linda Johnston, Auchrannie Resort

Campbeltown Machrihanish Tarbert Portavadie Loch Fyne Claonaig Lochranza Brodick River Spey

We had the ability to do all sorts of things. Our own arts organisation, Hi-Arts, for example and the Screen Machine… it was great. So dynamic. So exciting.

Iain Robertson,
HIE Chief Executive, 1991-2000

Co-founder and shareholder Linda Johnston arrived on the island from Irvine in 1983 when she was appointed PE teacher in the local school. She married Iain Johnston, a local retailer and property developer who was also Tourist Officer for Arran for a time, and together they bought Auchrannie as a 16-bedroom hotel which they wanted to turn into the kind of service-based luxury business that the island didn't yet have. Although their marriage didn't survive, the two remained business partners. "When we started Auchrannie 27 years ago," says Linda, "The island infrastructure was quite poor quality. We did give people a shake-up. Other people then began trying to improve quality too."

With help from HIE, Auchrannie has grown and grown. It is an example of a public and private co-operation that creates a boost not just to the local economy, but also to the sustainability of the island as a community. Linda has a very grounded, practical quality but also expresses a strong sense of the contribution she wants Auchrannie to make to the Island of Arran as a whole. It is important to her that the facilities it boasts, like the swimming pool, are open to locals as well as guests. "It's got to be for the community as well," she says.

A truly exceptional resort has been created at Auchrannie but it couldn't have been achieved with private investment alone. "There's no way we could have done it," acknowledges Linda. "We've had to borrow to complete each stage of our development." Is that daunting? "Not when you're confident in your product and have confidence in your financial team."

There have been frustrations as well as successes, she acknowledges. "There are difficulties reaching a stage of sustainability. For a time we were stuck, not making enough money to refurbish and redevelop. It was quite stressful." But then there was a cash injection to create the spa and new lodges and the cash that raised created new possibilities and pace to the development.

"It's all about passion and personality," says Richard Small, the chatty, high energy General Manager of Auchrannie. Richard started as a kitchen porter and has worked his way to the top there at the age of 41, via a stint at the Malmaison in Glasgow. "Linda and I are very passionate, even about fabrics and textiles, and hate things being the same as anywhere else. Every time we do something, we try to go above and beyond."

The majority of Auchrannie's business is repeat and referral. "To us, it's about giving people the wow factor and creating a product they want to come back to." To the extent, he says, that they are investing money in extra guest areas that have washing machines and microwaves and all the things that make guests feel at home. "We are unique in what we do. We put guest service first. We operate a very profitable business but people who come into the business can't believe how we operate. That's what makes us special. We constantly change, improve and advance what we deliver."

Businesses work together here to promote the island as a whole and have formed VisitArran, a destination management group. "There is collaboration," says Richard. "There's no competitive nastiness here. For example when the Douglas Hotel opened locally, people thought we would be unhappy but it's a completely different product and it brings more people to the island."

Community is particularly important on an island. "It's a nice place to live," says Linda. "You go to the hardware store for a scourer and emerge an hour and a half later."

"People look after one another," agrees Richard. "I have no dream of wanting to move. There's everything you need here. You might not have Marks and Spencer and night clubs but the culture, the way people live, the schools… it's all good and it's a safe environment for families."

In the restaurant of the Auchrannie, Sheila Gilmore, an ex-education officer who now works for VisitArran, is reminiscing about her childhood here

in the 1960s. She is an energetic, open woman who talks articulately and with such feeling that it makes you feel like you have known her for years. Her fingernails are painted in rainbow colours, each a different vibrant shade: sky blue and bright yellow and orange and hot pink. On her wrist, a red strap supports a Minnie Mouse watch.

"People didn't have a lot of money in the 1960s. Arran was quite hippy, cool, and trendy," she recalls. But that's not what people are looking for now. "People expect so much more. They want a better quality of experience. They want to come and be served." There are so many things for visitors to see. The Arran Distillery which is now open seven days a week. Arran Aromatics, a company that was started by Janet and Iain Russell in 1989, making soaps and body creams in their cottage kitchen using natural ingredients from the island. The many high quality food and drink manufacturers. And then, of course, the top quality accommodation.

"Auchrannie has been great for the whole island. People come all year round now. It's no longer a six week block in summer. The hotels are busy all the time and it has opened up the island. Yet, there are always people who object to development. Some objected to Auchrannie building a spa, says Sheila. Some objected to the building of a distillery. It's short sighted. "I would start a YIMBY association. Yes in My Back Yard."

There were 60-70 businesses signed up to VisitArran when Sheila started three years ago. Now there are 170.

Despite all the activity, the population of Arran is ageing. Schools rolls are falling. But there's optimism that can be turned round, says Sheila. The biggest difficulty facing young people is housing. "It's not employment. It's an employee's market on Arran with plenty of people looking for workers. Housing is the issue. People talk about low cost housing but it doesn't exist here. People in low cost housing are probably paying more than I am on my mortgage. I know I have been in my house a while but you know, it's really difficult for folk. I don't know what you do about that."

There are those who come on holiday to this idyllic island and want to live here. But even if they get a house, they don't always last. Things that seem quirky and charming when you are on holiday can begin to pall when you live there full time. For example HIE invested money in a "Screen Machine" for the Highlands and Islands, an 80-seat, air conditioned mobile cinema which brings the latest

Walker looking to Goat Fell at dawn

films to remote and rural areas. But there's only one and it has a vast area to cover.

"Island life is not for everyone," says Sheila. "Everything that is really good about it can also be its downside. When that boat goes it goes. You can't just say I'm going to pop out to Asda. The boat's gone. Pop out to the cinema? The Screen Machine is not here for another six weeks. People don't like it when the boat goes in the winter. It's a sense of isolation I suppose. It doesn't bother me because I was born and bred here and it's not an issue. For some people it is."

Sheila has a real sense of belonging to this island. She has run a drama club for youngsters for over 20 years and is past chairman of the island's drama association. She sits on the Highland Games committee, the ferry committee – you'll find her name on most sets of minutes that get circulated here.

"I would never live anywhere else because I am an Arran girl. I want to share that island with everybody. It's here," she says, touching her heart. "It's really corny but when I sail into Brodick Bay I think, I'm home. I have a sense of belonging. That's how I feel. I look at the hills and think… I'm just really lucky. I love it."

The CalMac ferry and Sheila Gilmore, Executive Director, VisitArran, at Brodick Harbour

Moray to **Inverness**

Late for a lunch date. A few wrong turns then, through dense green foliage on the road, the River Spey suddenly snakes ahead in a perfect channel. The road bends and the long driveway to Aberlour House appears, tucked securely into a corner. Tyres on gravel. An expanse of lawn. Serene stillness. The former Gordonstoun prep school is now the headquarters of Walkers, the Scottish bakers whose rich red tartan boxes of shortbread, biscuits, cakes and meringues are synonymous with Highland quality.

Inside the imposing grey stone house, Director Jim Walker shows me round the drawing room, explaining the pictures on the wall. Pride of place goes to Flora MacDonald captured in a 19th century painting by George William Joy. It's called 'Farewell to Prince Charlie' and the Young Pretender is depicted kissing Flora's hand in goodbye while she looks at him with wistful regret. Flora assisted the Prince's escape from the Hanoverian army after the 1745 rebellion and the iconic picture has appeared on Walkers shortbread tins for

many years. It was bought after Sothebys contacted the company in 1998 to inform them the painting had come up for sale. "It's the most romantic moment in Scottish history," says Jim.

Jim Walker is a grandson of the founder of Walkers and a true Highland gentleman. Tall and slim with white hair and dancing eyes, he has the personal warmth and gentle politeness of a generation that seems under threat. Yet he, his brother Joseph and sister Marjorie, also had the drive and dynamism that have taken Walkers from a small shop in the village of Aberlour in their father's day, to an international business. Joe was always a real genius in baking, whilst Jim was the company's first salesman.

Walkers now has an annual turn-over of £140 million and exports 40% of its production. It is the only food manufacturing company to win the Queen's Award for Export Achievement an incredible four times. The company

has offices in both Germany and the United States and also exports to Canada, Australia and the Far East, with the Japanese being particularly enthusiastic consumers of their crisp, all butter shortbreads and melt-in-the-mouth biscuits.

Up there on the wall is another Highland gentleman, Jim's grandfather Joseph, in a framed black and white photograph. Joseph trained as a baker and in 1898, at the age of 21, borrowed £50 to start his own business in the Torphins area of Aberdeenshire. A few years later he moved to a small shop on the main street of the picturesque village of Aberlour. Beneath the painting is Joseph's old desk, scratches revealing its age like wrinkles on a face. Jim remembers taking money to his grandfather at that desk. Propped on top is a framed card from the quintessential Scottish entertainer, Harry Lauder. Jim turns it over to show faded writing sloping across the card.

"I am confident Mrs Walker is the fruit cake queen," it says. But what about Mr Walker? What was his grandfather like? "He was quite a tough Scot," smiles Jim. "Very dour, canny and cautious – and reluctant to delegate authority."

And over here is the picture of his father, another James. Walkers is an increasingly rare example of a successful, truly independent, family-owned business. His grandfather handed on the business to his two sons James and Joseph. Joseph didn't have any children but James, Jim's father, had three. Marjorie is now retired but Jim and Joseph continue to work past retirement age for the company. Six of their children work for the company. Wouldn't Jim like to rest now? The company is too much in his blood, he replies.

"I think it's the huge pride I have in selling a product that I can genuinely say is the best in the world in its class," he explains. "There is pride in having your name on something that you know is better than others. I think what makes us different is our integrity. We don't need fancy copywriters. We just tell the truth. Our products are made with the finest raw ingredients and painstaking care in beautiful Speyside."

In the showroom of Aberlour house, an Aladdin's cave of red cartons opens up, an entire room of display shelves

with a quite incredible range of products. Shortbread with vanilla, with almond, and with ginger. Chocolate covered orange shortbread. Shortbread in the shape of Scottie dogs. Commemorative tins to mark royal occasions. Savoury oatcakes. Sweet meringues. Slabs of fruit cake topped with thick, yellow almond marzipan. Mince pies. Some of the shortbread products are crisp and some are crumbly. The variation in texture is achieved by using different proportions of just four basic ingredients: butter, sugar, flour and salt. "Four ingredients

everyone has in their kitchen," says Jim. "But the Scots put them together better than anyone else in the world."

Walkers products are luxury items, he says. They are not eaten every day and are often bought as gifts, particularly at Christmas. Their price range is therefore above basic supermarket prices but people are happy to pay a little extra for high quality and consistency. The company make products for upmarket supermarkets like Sainsburys, Waitrose and Marks and Spencer. But if

Jim and Joseph Walker

they tried to produce cheap biscuits, at bargain prices, they wouldn't be able to compete. "We can compete with anyone if it's quality you are looking for," explains Jim. "But we can't compete with the big companies on price."

Their distribution costs are higher than average and they also pay for fleets of buses to bring their 1,700 workers in each day from rural locations. It's a significant cost but paid without quibble.

It creates a loyal workforce and is, in any case, the company's contribution to the environment. "It saves 4 million road miles a year," says Jim. "When you grow up appreciating where you live, you want to preserve it. We are lucky to live in one of the most beautiful parts of the country." But communications have improved dramatically in this rural area. "We now have good air connections and good couriers. Someone in London can have a sample on their desk overnight. We can compete with anyone on service."

Moray, an area of stunning coastline and beaches, is famous for its high quality produce. Cashmere from Johnstons of Elgin, speciality food from Baxters and Walkers. Then there's whisky. In the few miles round Aberlour, the tall chimneys of the distilleries peep through trees at regular intervals. Aberlour, Glen Grant, Glenfiddich, Dailuaine, Cardhu, Macallan, Benrinnes, Glenrothes, Glenfarclas… Moray's 50 distilleries produce more of the world's malt whisky supply than the rest of the planet put together.

Walkers products

The distilleries, says Jim, employ mostly men. Walkers employs mostly women. Between the two, there is little unemployment in the Aberlour area. "We have a fantastic workforce with a real family atmosphere. We encourage people from the same families to work for us."

Sandwiches, and tea and coffee with china cups, are beautifully laid out on the showroom table for lunch but dessert is best: plates of Walkers biscuits. Try this one, says Jim, and this one. That one is crisp… that one is buttery… that one has chocolate… let me get you some dark chocolate… and so it goes on, a Mad Hatter tea party of deliciousness.

Down in the picturesque village of Aberlour, Joseph Walker's original shop is still there. It's also an experimental bakery now, allowing the company to test new recipes without closing down production lines in the main factory to bake them. The family name is still there, above the shop door, and after a visit to Aberlour House it's obvious how important that is. This company is all about history and heritage.

 "The ambition," says Jim, "is to keep Walkers independent, keep it in the family – and hand it over to the next generation in good shape."

Aberlour Distillery, Speyside

The A96 from Elgin to Inverness is the main road from Aberdeen that cuts through the small towns and villages of Moray before reaching Nairn, then finally Inverness. Inverness was granted city status in 2000 and it does not take long after arrival to discover what that means. Congested traffic. Car parks. Shopping malls. Once, this was a sleepy town where life meandered gently like its river and where locals tell you wryly that the pinnacle of their excitement was the day they heard that a branch of Marks and Spencer was opening. Now, most High Street names are represented in Inverness and research based on information from the Office of National Statistics, showed that in the ten years running up to 2008, the value of economic activity per person rose by 86% in the area – the highest rise in Scotland.

Looking at the scale of the Johnson & Johnson owned LifeScan Scotland building behind the security fences in Inverness, you are left in no doubt that something commercially important goes on here. Clearly, it's big business. All the more striking, then, when the friendly security guard accompanying me in the lift strikes up conversation. He's worked here for 12 years. "Great company to work for," he says. Security is now subcontracted, so strictly speaking, he's no longer an employee. "But we get treated the same as the staff," he says. Well that's good. "It's unheard of actually," he murmurs, almost to himself.

The statistics for LifeScan Scotland are impressive. The turnover in 2014 was £155 million; it's the biggest life sciences company in Scotland, employing over 1,000 people in the capital city of the Highlands; its revolutionary diabetes products – which monitor blood glucose levels – are at the forefront of world technology in the field; and the site is home to Johnson & Johnson's Self Monitoring of Blood Glucose (SMBG) research and development hub, which is constantly pushing the technology's accuracy and capabilities.

River Ness, Inverness

No successful region has an unsuccessful city at its heart. Fifty years ago, who would have thought there would be a university based in the Highlands and Islands? Who would have thought there would be LifeScan, one of the biggest life sciences companies in the world, working out of Inverness? That was inward investment that HIE secured for the region.

Willy Roe,
HIE Chairman, 2004-2012

A traditional music session taking place in the bar of Hootananny, Inverness

But sometimes, the human story tells you just as much. For example, the fact that the company has managed to encourage 80% of its workforce to participate in a health screening programme. All employees are entitled to fresh fruit each day and interestingly, the company has seen sales of fresh fruit increase in the staff canteen and sales of sugary snacks decrease as a result.

But it's not just the health of the workforce that LifeScan Scotland has influenced so positively; it's the health of the local economy. The deal bringing the factory to Inverness was struck in 1995 with a company called Inverness Medical Ltd, which was working in conjunction with Johnson & Johnson to create pioneering diagnostic products for people with diabetes.

Inverness is doing well.
We have to remember not all
areas have the same growth.

Alex Paterson,
HIE Chief Executive, 2010 to present

David McMillan, Managing Director, LifeScan Scotland

Highlands and Islands Enterprise saw the potential for the area and offered incentives to site the plant in Inverness. "HIE were truly instrumental in bringing the company here," acknowledges David McMillan, Managing Director, "The package they put together was the most attractive."

In return, the company has brought secure employment to the area. Johnson & Johnson bought the UK assets of Inverness Medical Ltd in 2001 at a time when the growth trajectory was off the scale. "The product couldn't satisfy market demand," explains David. Additional staff were taken on but it took until 2007 to clear back orders of their product, OneTouch® Ultra®. In the meantime, the company's research and development department continued to develop iterations and new technology, such as the OneTouch® Verio® product.

It is not just the product that has developed. The company has created a knowledge base in the Highland capital that is now world renowned. That expertise has led to an important collaboration between the National Health Service, the University of the Highlands and Islands, and LifeScan.

LifeScan Scotland, Inverness

The three partners work together at the Highland Diabetes Unit which is part of a new purpose-built Centre for Health Sciences, an initiative that was brokered by HIE in 2007.

In recent years, the Inverness site has attracted new operations that were previously done in the US. Johnson & Johnson's investment in the Highlands is at a stage that would be economically difficult to reverse and re-site. "The company has made a commitment here and continue to invest – the next manufacturing lines will be coming to Inverness," confirms David McMillan.

At one time, it would have been hard to believe that a world-leading science-based company and product could operate out of the Highlands. LifeScan Scotland proves it can be done.

The pitch was at a country club hotel in Ireland. I remember they put us into a room with the Irish who were pitching for it. There was also a pitch from the Israelis. We said we'd provide them with a building, grants, and training grants, and we'd support them through their development – and we did. We knew it had enormous potential.

Iain Robertson,
HIE Chief Executive, 1991-2000

For David McMillan, the solidifying of Inverness's position has enabled him to stay in an area that has offered an attractive quality of life. Originally from Musselburgh, near Edinburgh, he appreciates the natural advantages of Highland living. "Where else in the country can you live in a play park like this?" he asks.

Two of his staff, Ali and Malcolm, agree. Ali is originally from Aberdeen and worked as an airforce engineer in Kinloss for nine years before moving to Glasgow to work for Motorola. He now lives in Forres, Moray, a 40-minute drive away. "I came back because I love the area. The quality of life is great, Moray schools are great. People who move into the area are pleasantly surprised by what Inverness has to offer. There's this idea that it's the back of beyond but the reality is that it has a lot to offer. It's a very busy place with lots of restaurants, a major hub with a good atmosphere."

Plus, he says, the weather is good. "There's less rain and it's quite mild." It's not the usual perception of the frozen north. Malcolm, who is originally from Southampton, agrees. "There's a microclimate here."

Malcolm's aunt ran a boarding house in Boat of Garten, now part of the Cairngorms National Park, so he had

been in Scotland regularly before he moved here, but when he came for his LifeScan interview, it was his wife and children's first visit. "My wife loved it. She felt safe and secure walking round town. We've been here three years now and the kids are really happy in school which is so much better than their experience in England. We live on the outskirts of Inverness and everything is on our doorstep. We sold one of our cars and I now cycle to work. There's a cinema down the road, we can travel to Loch Ness or Fort William, go walking with the kids and the dog in the forest… we wouldn't move back."

Ali has worked for LifeScan for 10 years and can see the impact the company has had locally. "It's allowed a technology base in Inverness that wasn't there before. I thought I'd have to work in Aberdeen for a career in energy and science." The company has also won an award for its encouragement of the modern apprenticeship scheme and has an on-site graduate programme.

There are geographical challenges, Ali admits. But Inverness has air links to London, Belfast, Dublin and Amsterdam. "The air links are important. It's vital for us that we maintain strong links with the rest of the company." It's also important to establish strong contacts in emerging markets in electronics across Europe and

Asia. "India is now a hotbed. For our cost base to be effective we have to work with these people and we must maintain links."

Both Ali and Malcolm are committed to meeting the challenges. "I'd struggle to find a company so good to work for," admits Ali. But it's more than the company. "If anything happened, I wouldn't be looking to move away," he continues. Both men have friends whose jobs have taken them to London but who refuse to shift their base from the Highlands, preferring to travel home at weekends. Both understand that thinking. "My wife," says Malcolm, "says if anything happens to this place, we're staying here."

A group of walkers crossing a snowy plateau in the Cairngorms National Park

When Fiona Larg was growing up in the small rural community of Stratherrick in the 1960s, the transition from primary to secondary school was traumatic. The nearest school was Inverness and in those days, the 18-mile journey was considered too far to travel daily. The roads were too bad, the winters too severe. Instead, Fiona had to stay in a hostel.

"I was only 11 years old and it was horrendous," she recalls. "It was the worst period of my life."

The child who had to leave home just to get to secondary school is now Chief Operating Officer and Secretary for the

Fiona Larg, Chief Operating Officer and Secretary, University of the Highlands and Islands

University of the Highlands and Islands. Back then, it would have been hard to believe such an institution would ever exist but Inverness, which is now a city with a population of almost 70,000, was a very different place. "Inverness had a population of about 30,000 then. It was a small town, very parochial. We had a Woolworths – and that was a big deal."

Fiona graduated as a chartered accountant and returned to the Highlands only as a temporary secondment to HIDB from her job in Glasgow. Her father had died a couple of years before and her mother was struggling to run the family shop, so she was travelling north regularly at weekends anyway. When asked to take the secondment, it seemed like a good temporary measure that would help her mother. It was summertime and she was sent to Skye. "I thought, my God, I'm getting paid to drive to Skye in the sunshine. It seemed like the job from heaven, especially at that time of year. It was incredibly liberating after being in a chartered accountancy office."

Fiona stayed and eventually went on to become Chief Executive of the Local Enterprise Company, Inverness and Nairn Enterprise. She knows from her former job trying to attract investors to the area how significant the development of a university is to the Highlands and Islands. "One of the biggest stumbling blocks in attracting big business was

The growth of the university sector is going to be important going forward. The University of the Highlands and Islands is central to this – a top priority – and we must tap into wider expertise that can benefit the region.

Alex Paterson,
HIE Chief Executive, 2010 to present

that they would ask what university, what research facilities, do you have? Where do we get graduates from?"

In 1967 when Fiona was a child, Scotland was on the point of gaining a new university. Inverness applied but was rejected along with Dumfries, Ayr, Falkirk, Perth and Cumbernauld, with Stirling being announced the victor. The prospect of a Highland-based university disappeared for more than a generation.

One name is mentioned repeatedly and with great affection when the origins of the University of the Highlands and Islands (UHI), and the campaign to have it set up, are recounted. The late Bob Cowan, the last chairman of HIDB and the first of HIE, was instrumental in ensuring that the idea of a Highlands and Islands university was kept alive.

A university is a fundamental part of successful communities around the world. The people it brings to both teach and learn are stimulating for the whole region… the status it brings the area… the confidence it brings. Confidence is a hugely important factor in successfully stimulating an economy. It has to be sustained and grown over generations.

Sir Fraser Morrison,
HIE Chairman, 1992-1998

University of the Highlands and Islands graduation

*UHI was a joint venture,
a great example of how
HIE could motivate others,
but Bob Cowan was
the original driver.
Lots of credit should go to him.*

Iain Robertson,
HIE Chief Executive, 1991-2000

"He was an amazing man to work with," says Fiona. "He and Val MacIver, Head of Education at the Council at the time, worked together to get a university established. This was a huge area of depopulation for 16-30 year olds and graduates were not coming back. There was a missing generation. They felt if they could create a university in the Highlands and Islands, it would address that. The University of the Highlands and Islands has a unique structure. It is not a single campus university but uses an existing network of 13 further education colleges across the HIE region, as well as Perth. A major new campus has been built at Inverness where further and higher education co-exist. Students can stay in their existing areas and make use of their local colleges, plus UHI's sophisticated video conferencing facilities.

UHI was finally granted university status in 2011 and it is estimated that around 75% of its students are from the catchment area of the Highlands and Islands with 18% from the rest of Scotland and the remainder from abroad. "It allows people the choice of staying in their local community," says Fiona, "maybe for caring responsibilities or financial considerations. There's a long history of people in the Highlands and Islands going off to university and being so unhappy away from home that they gave up."

It's not just about retaining young people but attracting them, allowing a free flow in and out of the region. The university is not solely about education; it's about research and development, about attracting new businesses and new projects to the Highlands and Islands that will make the area grow and thrive. HIE has developed and will have a presence at the heart of the new Inverness Campus, reflecting this important collaboration between education and industry. The development agency will co-locate with key research and education departments from the university and will provide a nationally and internationally significant location for business, research and education.

Inverness has grown beyond recognition in the last 50 years. It was always the Highland HQ for public bodies like the Council, the NHS, the police and fire services, and therefore depended heavily on public sector employment. But its fortunes have changed with significant private inward investment. The university has the potential to consolidate that development. As the American writer, Anthony J D'Angelo put it, "Develop a passion for learning. If you do, you will never cease to grow."

North to **Caithness, Orkney and Shetland**

White space. Light streams through doors and windows. White walls and white sofas and a white bird cage with an artificial parrot. Stags' heads. A mannequin. Stacked boxes with labels. Paints and brushes and an easel. The house is tucked behind greenery at the end of a cul de sac in an ordinary residential area of Inverness. But in here it's Alice down the rabbit hole; Alice through the looking glass; the wardrobe door to Narnia. It's a working space but an interesting one, where quirky style meets creativity, and the detritus of art and design tells the story of what happens within these studio walls.

Sandra Murray works from home yet has dressed the Queen. Commissioned to make an outfit for the monarch for the opening of the Scottish Parliament in 1999, her bespoke, high-end designs subsequently reached a whole new audience. "A commission like that is quite major and I got a lot of work on the back of it," she says, her soft island accent revealing her Stornoway origins. "People who gave me a hard time suddenly became my best pals!"

When we meet, Sandra is dressed in one of her own creations, a stylish black pinstripe trousers-and-skirt-in-one design that she made but has teamed with a crisp, white cotton ruffled shirt she bought. She considers herself an artist first and a designer and dressmaker second. She makes garments in the way an artist creates paintings: because she has a vision and she loves it. Selling comes second for those pieces.

Her portfolio shows a series of stunning tartan dresses, a union of traditional patterns with innovative designs that cascade with ruffles and flounces and asymmetric lines. Her clothes have an inherent drama, a style beyond fashion, and are often created in colours that have been influenced by nature. "I was brought up in a rustic environment. I like muted colours and I'm big on texture."

In addition to tartans and tweeds, Sandra uses exotic fabrics that she sources herself and goes abroad to buy: froths of French lace, Italian chiffon, fine satins and silks, and rich velvets. She brings out a gown that she has made but is yet to sell, a beautiful, soft, flowing dress in soft greys, the colours of a stormy sky. You could imagine a Keira Knightley wearing it, someone with the bone structure to carry such delicacy. With pieces like this, she doesn't find a customer and then make the garment; she makes the garment because she wants to, then finds a customer who wants it enough to buy it.

"I mind who wears it," she admits. She wants someone who loves the artistry of it. "I want someone who approaches it in the way a collector would, or the way a museum curator would."

Left: Sandra Murray design, Loch Ness
Right: Sandra Murray

It wasn't always this way. Before she entered the world of up-market design, she had many years of producing bread-and-butter creations to make a living.
She graduated from art school in 1974 and at first thought she wanted to be a teacher. "But I was very unhappy," she admits. She started making clothes, mainly for businessmen's wives, and her business really got going through word of mouth and reputation. But she struggled with some aspects of running her own business.
"I wasn't a business person; I was creative," she admits. "I was learning as I went along. I was subsidising my income with two days teaching a week and the business was evolving all the time."

There is a perception that HIE only assist businesses which employ a lot of people. But if a small business offers something unique, they can win backing. Sandra Murray is an example of a solo operator who was supported by HIE to establish and run a small creative business that is deeply rooted in, and inspired by, the region's textures, tones and Gaelic culture, yet trades worldwide to a highly valuable and specialised market. Her website can be viewed in English, Japanese and Gaelic, reflecting her key global audiences.

For Sandra, the problem was finding the right niche market. She decided to make a ready-to-wear line of ladies' tweed jackets to sell to exclusive outlets like House of Bruar and Johnstons of Elgin but it became a challenge. "The problem is these places want thousands of garments. Over four years, I must have done a few hundred. Trying to do ready-to-wear wasn't viable because of the logistics."

She knew she was good at recognising what suited people and designing for them accordingly. But she also wanted to pursue the side of herself that had trained as an artist. One day she heard the Chief Executive of a big company talking on the radio. He was asked if price was important. He said yes, unless you are in the market above that where it's about the product and not the price. Sandra listened intently. "I wanted to sell to a high-end network. I wanted to become a specialist."

She had reached a turning point and knew she needed to rebrand. "I thought I'd reached a glass ceiling. I had to change direction. As an artist, I have to make things and find a customer for that. I knew the price had to go up if it was going to be viable. It's like playing chess… what's the next move?" The photo-shoot in her portfolio cost £20,000 and HIE, alongside Scottish Development International, contributed to the preparatory costs and travel to New York to build a presence to allow her access to the markets she needed. It's more satisfying, she says,

selling something exclusive for £25,000 to one person than something cheaper to lots of different people. People pay for something unique. "I use fabrics that are not easy to source. I am pretty specialised in the UK, not just in Scotland."

Does she ever doubt that her product is worth the price tag? "I don't question it. I have been sewing since I was 10 and I am now 63. That's 50 years on the job, hands-on experience. I travel a lot, go to shops a lot. I know the level my own product is at. I was watching a film about Dior recently. There's nothing happening there that's not happening here. It's just that they have a team of 100 making the clothes and I make everything. That takes a lot of experience."

Her customers are found through talking personally to people and through word of mouth. "I have to find my own customer, talk to a lot of people, get referrals. My target is finding the person who appreciates what I do. But it's no good having a room full of people who admire your stuff. You need a few who can afford it. It's like a dog sniffing out truffles. It's under cover but you sniff it out."

And the Queen? Sandra thinks it goes back to a customer from 15 years before the commission actually came her way. You never know, she says, the repercussions of something. Or how the customer will react to the finished product, of course. "I met the Queen about four times. I sent the portfolio, had the cloth made, then went to both Windsor and Buckingham Palace. She put it on and said, 'Splendid,' – and that was it."

Recently, Sandra heard Natalie Massenet of the internationally famous chain Net-a-Porter speaking. Massenet said she would love to dress the Queen. In a studio in a quiet cul-de-sac of Inverness, Sandra Murray has already ticked that box.

The Kessock Bridge arches ahead, heralding the exit out of Inverness and the continuation of the A9 north. The light is often beautiful here in the early evening,

the sky on fire, flooded with red and pink and orange, or the sun streaming through greyness onto the water in a perfect shaft of light, as if beamed from some heavenly projector located somewhere behind the dense clouds. Other times the colour is washed gently; grey blue and lavender, soft and muted, shrouding the hills softly, creeping insidiously round the landscape.

Kessock Bridge, Inverness

> *Inverness is a city with a university and a football team. None of that existed when I was growing up. It's fundamentally different.*
>
> **Sir Fraser Morrison,**
> HIE Chairman, 1992-1998

As you cross the bridge, Inverness Caledonian Thistle (ICT) Football Club is visible on the right, the three-sided stadium tucked into a cold corner down by the sea, where the wind whips up from the Beauly Firth. Like Ross County, ICT is now in the Scottish Premier League. Two Highland Premier League football clubs would have once been unthinkable – and was unwanted by some. Back in 1997, there was a vacancy in the Scottish League because of restructuring. At the time, Inverness had three football teams in the Highland League. Back then, I wrote a story for my newspaper about merger plans for the clubs in order to give them the strength to make it into the Scottish League. In the teams' social clubs, die-hard fans frowned into their beers and were vociferous in their opposition. They'd never follow a new Inverness team if their club died in the merger, they vowed. Almost 20 years later, some still won't.

The merger went ahead. Fiona Larg can smile about it now, but back then she was Chief Executive of Inverness and Nairn Enterprise and has reason to remember the opposition. Fiona wanted to ensure Inverness didn't lose out if all three Highland League clubs competed for one place but merger wasn't an easy journey. One of the clubs wouldn't even allow her to attend their board meetings. No women allowed.

Times change. Inverness Clach dropped out of the merger but in 1994, Inverness Caledonian and Inverness Thistle combined to become Caledonian Thistle, later Inverness Caledonian Thistle. Fiona's high profile intervention made her the target for disgruntled fans. They even tried legal moves to block the merger. "I used to get phone calls at one in the morning," she recalls. "We know where you live!"

A man came into the office reception one day, dressed in a leather jacket, his hand tucked into the inside pocket. "I thought, I don't like the look of this," recalls Fiona. "I got the biggest guy in the office to find out what he wanted. He said, 'I want Fiona Larg. She's ruined my life.' I unleashed feelings and emotions I didn't even know existed." The man, who was escorted from the premises, obviously subscribed to the Bill Shankly school of football: Football a matter of life and death? No, far more important than that.

Inverness Caledonian Thistle moved rapidly from the third division, to the second, to the first, and in 2004 made it to the Premier League. Along the way, memorable victories against Celtic earned them a reputation as giant slayers and led to a famous sporting headline in the Sun that captured the imagination of sports fans across the country: "Super Caley Go Ballistic, Celtic Are Atrocious."

Scottish Premier League football is in economically challenging times but Inverness Caledonian Thistle has gone on to be one of its success stories.

In 2015, the club won the Scottish Cup. Inverness Caledonian Thistle v Ross County is the Highland equivalent of an Old Firm match with lots of rivalry but little venom. "Winning the cup was a fantastic achievement," acknowledges Steven Ferguson of Ross County. "Nobody can take that away from them." For everyone, it was a sign that Highland football had truly arrived.

Inverness Caledonian Thistle, winners of the 2015 Scottish Cup

Nigg juts into the sea, the chin of the landscape, little more than a point of land that served as the ferry terminal for boats from the historic town of Cromarty across the water. It can be reached by road from Inverness but a drive through the peninsula of the Black Isle to take the ferry at Cromarty opens up rich, rolling farmland and a chance to dolphin watch at Chanonry Point near Fortrose. The summer ferry crossing from Cromarty takes just a few minutes. On the other side, there was little at Nigg from 2000 until 2011 to demonstrate the huge significance of this place to the Highland economy. In its heyday, the flat expanse of land was a powerhouse of the oil industry, with thousands of workers occupying the site.

Back in 1972, Archie McCreevy sat outside the main gate of the yard watching the comings and goings, the stream of lorries that were carrying materials to develop the site that was to support the construction of North Sea oil platforms. He wanted a job there. As he approached the security gate, he was stopped. Did he have a letter for the supervisor? He didn't. Archie asked the name of the supervisors he needed to see and then sat in his car, watching the lorries. They turned into another gate, and when he got the chance, he swung his car in behind the convoy – and gained entry another way.

A job was his. Originally from Glencoe, Archie had trained as an electrician and was taken on as one of a team of 160 sparks employed in the development phase of the yard. One of the most important questions he was asked was if he had proof that he had living accommodation.

Nigg Energy Park

There were so many workers on the site that there was not enough local housing and men were sharing three to a room in places – and were grateful to do so. "People were living in garden sheds and caravans," says Archie, who went on to work at the nearby Invergordon aluminium smelter.

Energy has played a significant part in the economic development of the Highlands and Islands. Large scale hydroelectric schemes were developed throughout the 1940s, 50s and 60s, providing the bedrock for a modern economy and stimulating the development of construction, transport and engineering firms that would support the explosion of the oil and gas industries in the 1970s. Then there was the nuclear fast reactor at Dounreay which opened in the early 1970s. Dounreay is no longer active but an extensive decommissioning process was started in 1998 and Dounreay still supports a substantial workforce of 2,000, plus an associated supply chain, and is expected to do so until the early 2020s.

Nigg and the Port of Ardersier were the powerhouses of the oil industry, along with Arnish in the Outer Hebrides (also known as the Western Isles), Kishorn and Argyll. The first oil platform, Highland One, was built in a huge dry dock at Nigg. The steel structure was then floated out to the Cromarty Firth, towed out to sea and piled into the sea bed. It was a huge project, the largest in the North Sea, and the start of a new energy chapter for the Highlands and Islands. "There was plenty of talk and excitement but we didn't know it was the beginning of an era," reflects Archie. "The dock was created to build two platforms, Highland One and Highland Two – but demand created otherwise."

> *The extent of our natural resources and the potential to exploit them are hugely exciting... renewable energy is one of our biggest growth opportunities.*

Lorne Crerar,
HIE Chairman, 2012 to present

The major North Sea skill was welding and local people were taken on and retrained for the industry. "It ended up with 8,000 people at Nigg and the site couldn't handle it," explains Archie. "There were too many people and it was a logistical nightmare. There was lots of money and it was spent freely in the community. They even had to put a police station on the site which the company financed."

There would be 20 years of employment in the fabrication yards but gradually, technology in the industry changed and oil platforms became smaller. Huge sites like Nigg became unnecessary. "The platforms became almost like IKEA platforms – home assembly!" says Archie. They were constructed in sections in the Middle East and sunk into the sea bed, bit by bit. The Highland yards went onto a care and maintenance basis, the ghosts of the good times blowing round the empty sites. Young workers headed offshore. "Needs must when the devil drives," says Archie.

Despite change and development, the oil industry continues to thrive. More than half of North Sea reserves are still to be extracted. In 2011, Nigg was re-opened by Global Energy Group to support the inspection, repair and upgrade of mobile drilling and marine assets in the Scottish oil industry. With HIE support, the company has invested over £40 million

Global Energy Group

Inverness   Cromarty   Nigg   Alness   Invergordon   Wick   John O'Groats   Pentland Firth   Orkney   Shetland

Alness transformed itself and the real reason was that the community took control. We brought jobs but they brought community spirit. Was winning Britain in Bloom important? It was crucially important. It was a small Highland town regaining its pride and identity. It was saying, we are a beautiful town, a place to live and bring up children.

Sandy Cumming,
HIE Chief Executive, 2000-2010

to create one of Europe's most modern energy facilities. The site now employs around 800 people, and is fast becoming a hub for the Scottish marine renewables and offshore wind industries.

HIE has invested continually in the support of one of the area's key assets: renewable energy. In 1982, HIE invested in the UK's first community based wind power scheme, with diesel backup, on Fair Isle in Shetland, and since then the industry has grown and developed. The wildness of the weather in the more remote parts of the north make this an energy rich area with enormous potential for wind power, both offshore and onshore, and also wave and tidal energy. By 2011, 35% of Scotland's electricity demand was being met by green energy with the Highlands and Islands making a substantial contribution. The target for 2015 is to meet 50% of demand, and the industry expects this to be easily reached.

The road north to Nigg runs past Alness. The small Ross-shire town could easily seem like a grey, one-street wonder if it were not for the care and attention lavished on it to make it bright and attractive. In summer it's a waterfall of colour, flowers arching gracefully from a multitude of hanging baskets that line the main street and have brought the town a win in the 'Britain in Bloom' competition. In the 90s, this area was an unemployment blackspot with the aluminium smelter,

which supported 1,100 jobs, closing in the nearby town of Invergordon. HIE took the brave decision to build advance offices here in the hope of encouraging businesses to move in. British Telecom did, bringing over 300 jobs to the area.

Heading north from Alness, it's on past Invergordon, a deep sea port that plays host to a mix of cruise liners visiting the Highlands, and oil rigs that are being refurbished and maintained. Then the road twists and turns up into Caithness and Sutherland, an area of wild, mountainous beauty that also contains the Flow country, the largest expanse of blanket bog in Europe. The bog areas and the soaring cliff tops at the dramatic coastal areas nurture unique bird communities, including golden plovers and dunlins, greenshanks and curlews, peregrine and golden eagles. Local community groups and the RSPB have created a network of museums and interpretive centres across the north, explaining the area's natural and cultural history to its many visitors.
The area also hosts the annual Lairg sheep sale – Europe's largest one-day auction of hill sheep and lambs.

Easter Ross is part of the North Coast 500 road trip, Scotland's answer to the USA's Route 66. It runs north from Inverness to John O'Groats, west along the powerful scenery of North Sutherland to Cape Wrath, then turns south through some of the most dramatic landscapes in Europe

The Highlands and Islands is the obvious place for renewable energy and the opportunities are huge. Some of the best green technology and know-how in the world is in this region. If we can make it happen, there's a real international opportunity for us in this sector.

Alex Paterson,
HIE Chief Executive, 2010 to present

to Ullapool in Wester Ross. The small, picturesque harbour town is ferry gateway to the Outer Hebrides and home to one of the UK's most alternative music festivals, Loopallu. Only 2,500 people attend the festival each year – effectively doubling Ullapool's population – yet it attracts big name acts from the cream of the British music scene.

It's remote and beautiful territory and as you pass mile after mile of deserted landscape, you can't help wondering how this area supports communities, what there is to hold and sustain the young people who grow up here. In the imposing grey stone building of the old Wick High School, Computing Science teacher, Chris Aitken is making his mark in that regard, encouraging the young people in his classes to compete with anyone, anywhere in the world. For four consecutive years, his computing science teams from this most northerly area of the mainland have won the national UK competition, "Apps for Good", which encourages young people to identify a problem in their community or their world, then create an app to solve it. "They design a solution, then do research and a business plan, work on a prototype, and enter the competition," explains Chris. "Last year, 22,000 students nationally took part."

To win once is a huge achievement. Four times in a row, particularly in an area

where, until now, internet connection has been variable, is extraordinary. Chris wants his students to have as much industry experience as possible and has also encouraged them to take part in everything that will give them experience of the wider world. He has organised volunteering expeditions to Belize and to Spain for his pupils, raising over £50,000 towards costs. "It's about seeking opportunities for them," he says. "Making them believe."

His thinking, he says, was influenced by Bob McDowell, the Vice President of Microsoft. On a visit to Scotland, McDowell was persuaded to fly north to address the pupils of Wick Academy. On a windswept day in Caithness, they assembled ready to hear his address but McDowell's flight was delayed. He arrived, delivered his speech, and left half an hour later because of his tight schedule. But the impact of that brief visit lived on. "He said you are not disadvantaged because of your location," explains Chris. "He said you can compete with anyone in the world because of the internet. I have never forgotten it."

Chris was born and brought up in Wick and returned to teach here because he didn't want to live anywhere else. "Even when I was in Aberdeen, my heart was still in Caithness. I just love the place. My family were here, parents and grandparents and great-grandparents.

It's just a great place to be. Some see it as a bleak landscape but it has so many different types. There's the Caithness Coast where you never know when you'll come on an old ruined castle, the inland mountains… Then there's Loch More. It's such a diverse landscape, beautiful in its starkness."

He recognises, though, the limitations that a remote location can put on young minds. When he left school with only one Higher, he didn't know what he wanted to do with his life. He took a job at a BT call centre and discovered he had a skill. He was good with computers. He understood them. Chris returned to study, eventually emerging with a First Class Honours degree from Aberdeen University. Despite being top of his class, he didn't have much industry experience. Does he regret not making the breakthrough? "Every day – but there's no point in dwelling on it. Besides, he's content teaching, loves opening up doors for his pupils. "I couldn't get a better job in a better place. Just as long as I can push the next generation to have that industry connection…"

His work has resulted in 80% of senior students taking computing science in Wick High School with more girls than ever opting for the subject. "The breakdown is now 60% boys and 40% girls so the 50-50 split is getting closer," he says.

Chris Aitken, Wick High School

Natural Retreats' refurbished Inn at John O'Groats
and Norse style tourist accommodation

His pupils have won many competitions, including one to visit Microsoft in Atlanta, Georgia. He also sends one of Wick's best students down to London each year to work as an intern for Thompson Reuters. "They come back as different kids because of the London experience, confident in what they do." Bob McDowell's words inform everything he does with his pupils. "Our kids are running with these opportunities. Some kids are studying in the Arctic, one climbed Kilimanjaro, one volunteered in Tanzania. They realise they can achieve, that they have the skills and ability to take part and compete."

At John O'Groats, the Pentland Firth stretches ahead, separating the mainland from the 70 islands of Orkney and further on, the islands of Shetland. Orkney, green and rolling, can surprise visitors used to the mountains and moors of the Highlands. In fact it has some of the best farming land in the north, producing excellent grass and cattle. Orkney beef is a premium brand, as is its salmon, crabmeat and whiskies, all of which are exported all over the world. The natural richness of the islands made it a magnet for Norse settlers twelve hundred years ago, who made Orkney the centre of a North Atlantic Earldom that dominated the region for hundreds of years. The islands are known for their ancient magic and are home to some of the world's best preserved Neolithic sites, Bronze Age cemeteries, Viking ruins, medieval castles, sunken German battleships from WWI, and Britain's most northerly cathedral, founded in 1137. It's easy to see why Orkney is one of Scotland's most popular visitor attractions.

Both Orkney and Shetland have their place in Scotland's more recent history too. Large oil terminals were built at Flotta on Orkney and Sullom Voe on Shetland and the communities have benefited from the major source of revenue ever since. A multi-million pound investment by BP and Total has secured the oil industry there for the next 30 years.

Standing in front of the impressively refurbished Inn at John O'Groats you can see the power that is created as the wind whips across the Pentland Firth, meeting the onrushing tide, causing whirlpools, standing waves and powerful tidal races. Locals have names for them, such as the 'Merry Men of Mey'. Mariners regard them with deep respect. From John O'Groats the most impressive are the surges of water that crash thunderously over the cliffs of the deserted island of Stroma, as the Atlantic Ocean rushes to meet the North Sea. This is dramatic evidence of the power of the sea that is being harnessed through the world's first commercial-scale tidal stream array – a farm of undersea turbines a mile or so offshore from the late Queen Mother's Castle of Mey. The MeyGen project, which aims to contribute up to 400MW of predictable, carbon-free clean electricity to the National Grid, is on track to produce its first power in 2016.

Over on Orkney itself, the European Marine Energy Centre (EMEC) is the only place of its kind in the world, an innovative centre which tests full-scale grid-connected prototype devices for marine energy projects in unrivalled wave and tidal conditions. The project will lead to the investment of hundreds of millions of pounds in the next ten years.

Neil Kermode moved from Bournemouth to Orkney to become Managing Director of EMEC. A trained civil engineer, he describes it as "the best job in the world".

Neil Kermode, Managing Director, EMEC

OpenHydro tidal turbine undergoing testing at EMEC

Living in Orkney has been refreshing. "The main culture shock in coming to Orkney was the way people engage with new ideas. It's such a breath of fresh air. Their attitude is, 'Yes and…' not, 'No, but…'. People want to make things happen on Orkney. It's very powerful."

You couldn't have EMEC in the south of England, he says. "There would be too many people sticking their oar in!" The openness of the Orcadians to innovation is partly, he suggests, the impact of living on an island and having to be resourceful. "There's a cultural acceptance that it's not about absolute knowledge, or the right to do things in a certain way. Ideas are washed up like driftwood on the beach and there's a willingness to look at new things that come along."

Cables at the test site run from a depth of 50 metres out in the sea onto the shore and are connected to the National Grid. Then the test devices are plugged in and the amount of electricity they generate at sea is measured onshore. Devices from all over the world have been tested on Orkney, using both wave energy and tidal energy. Wave energy essentially uses old wind energy, the power created when the wind blows across the surface of the water, whereas tidal energy is driven by planetary movement, the gravitational effect of the sun and moon.

Has the technology been proved? Not quite enough to compete on cost yet, admits Neil. "But these technologies often take quite a period of time to reach technical maturity. The kit does work.

You can make electricity out of sea water and we have proved that. What we haven't proved yet is that it is reliable and cheap enough to afford. We have to make this cheaper than oil and gas and we are a way off yet."

But he has no doubt that the potential is there. It's quite simple. Standing looking at the crashing waters of the Pentland Firth, the waves frothing at the edges like they sport white lace frills, the signs are obvious. "You only have to stand on the shore in Orkney and feel the waves crashing in to know there's a shed load of energy here," says Neil.

A shed load of energy. It's in the sea and in the people of these islands. It's in their spirit, a spirit born from resilience, innovation and creativity. There is something about the landscape, the space, the light, the essence of the Highlands and Islands, that inspires creativity in artists, musicians and writers. From Orkney, whose illustrious writers include George Mackay Brown and Edwin Morgan, it is just a hop and a skip to Shetland which lies 100 miles north of the mainland of Scotland and consists of 100 islands. It is an area of rolling hills and rocky coastlines, towering cliffs and sandy coves – and the sea, always the sea. You are never more than three miles from water on Shetland, the tumultuous energy of crashing waves in winter, or the sleeping lion calm of spring and summer tides.

Shetland's days of struggle – an inevitable part of remote communities – ended with the arrival of the oil industry in the 1970s, and the construction of the oil terminal at Sullom Voe. The ways in which the people of Shetland took control of the industry, carved out a future for their islands, and invested the fruits in their community's infrastructure, has made this a dynamic and thriving place to live with many economic and artistic opportunities. When the HIDB was set up in 1965, it was Shetland and its fishing and knitwear industries that made the biggest demands on the fledgling development agency's budget. With the support of grants and

loans from HIDB, fishermen were able to invest in new and bigger boats, creating a vibrant whitefish industry in a few short years. It was a thriving local economy, built on a real partnership between the community and the support agency, that allowed Shetland to look multinational oil companies in the eye and demand real local benefit.

Modern Shetland is a place of contrasts, boasting a road, ferry and community hall network that is the envy of the rest of the Highlands and Islands, yet with two islands, Foula and Fair Isle, wholly dependent on locally managed renewable energy systems to provide electricity for everyday needs. Fair Isle is famous for its bird observatory, which draws ornithologists from all over the world, and Foula is equally renowned as Britain's most remote inhabited island. It was the location for Michael Powell's 1937 film The Edge of the World, standing in for St Kilda. Eighty years on, it's still home to a small but determined crofting community.

The capital, Lerwick, is a real North Atlantic town, with a flag stone paved main street winding past traditional stone shops and homes – some with their own piers and jetties – before opening out into an extensive modern harbour stretching north for several miles. Enormous pelagic fishing boats, big enough to catch a whole shoal of

herring or mackerel in minutes, jostle for space with cruise ships, oil supply vessels, and cargo boats en route to the Faroes. Darting between these workhorses of the oil and fishing industry, are small traditional 'yoals' rowed by a crew of six, practising for the frequent local races, with competitions for both men and women. Clearly descended from Viking longships, these yoals demonstrate, along with the annual Up Helly Aa fire festival, the determination of Shetland to celebrate their Norse heritage while embracing the 21st Century.

Up Helly Aa, Lerwick

Davie Gardner, who runs Atlantic Edge Music Services on Shetland, represents different strands of the unique energy that exists on the Shetland Isles: oil and the arts. But he remembers when things were different. In the 1970s, he took on an apprenticeship at a local paper but gave it up to work in the developing oil industry which was breathing new life into the area. "In the 50s and 60s this was a much more rural community," explains Davie. "There was no TV until 1964 and even then there was only one channel. The opportunities for young people were very few and if you had any ambition, you had to leave Shetland. It was the oil industry that changed that." Davie worked for the Lerwick Harbour Trust and as an operations supervisor for Shell UK before taking voluntary redundancy. He had always loved music and was used to doing occasional freelance work for BBC Radio Shetland, making up packages

Left: Sullom Voe oil and gas terminal
Right: Davie Gardner

and contributing interviews for music programmes. "Music is a huge part of Shetland culture. It's engrained in the community," he says. So when he received a call from the BBC after leaving his day job, he was delighted to hear that they wanted him to contribute more regularly. It was full circle, coming back to the journalism he had wanted to pursue as a teenager, and the timing could not have been better. He was being offered the chance to make a living out of his personal passion. "I loved music but didn't play an instrument so knew I would never be a musician.

I started promoting concerts instead. I promote anything I like that is good quality, from traditional to rap music. It's a huge passion."

In 1997, he took on the job of music adviser to Shetland Arts Trust, staying in the job for eight years and progressing a whole range of initiatives that included event promotion, youth music projects, and working with musicians to promote their music internationally. He even won a Scottish Thistle award, normally a tourist industry accolade, for a music project that included

There is a dynamic arts and cultural scene in the Highlands and Islands and HIE has always supported this. Our role in increasing cultural vibrancy and nurturing creative clusters has certainly helped drive economic growth.

Willy Roe,
HIE Chairman, 2004-2012

a tourism element. By the time he left the job in 2006, he had worked to bring Elvis Costello, Ian Brown of the Stone Roses, Steve Earle and Kris Kristofferson to the Shetland Isles.

Just 24 hours after he left the security of a full-time job to freelance for the second time, he received a call from a member of what is now one of Shetland's best known traditional music bands, Fiddlers' Bid. Did Davie fancy being their agent and manager? It was a move that was to move his business up a gear, lead him to another successful local group, Bodega, and take him to America, Canada, Australia and Japan.

Now his business has diversified. Davie not only promotes music gigs, he also acts as a TV and film facilitator, a 'fixer' who seeks out locations suitable for film and television productions on the islands. He was involved in the famous 'Moonwalking Shetland Pony' advert, and with providing locations for the television adaptation of the books of local Shetland author, Ann Cleeves. Cleeves' novels about a Shetland detective, Jimmy Perez, have been made into a series with the lead being played by Scottish actor Dougie Henshall.

Concert promoter, film fixer, broadcaster, feature writer for a local magazine…there's nothing Davie won't consider. "Anything I can turn my mind to, I do," he says, summing up the entrepreneurial opportunism necessary when trying to make a living in a small community. "It's all about being able to tie in to the community and culture of Shetland and using that to your own advantage – but giving something back too."

Eshaness, Shetland

By air to **the Outer Hebrides**

The Harris Tweed Hebrides mill at Shawbost on the Isle of Lewis is like a Willy Wonka factory for textiles. Bags of pure virgin wool in the shades of rainbow sweeties lie ready for mixing into colourful confections: yellow, candy pink, orange, magenta. Once blended, the colours become softer, more muted, the colours of island lochs and rain and earth and heather. And the noise! Wheels spin and chains turn and pistons pump and the air is filled with banging and clanking while puffs of wool emerge in glass chambers like exotic coloured candy floss before being tamed, combed, wound and spun.

It's been an early flight from Inverness to Stornoway, a red summer dawn staining the Highland capital's sky. A mere hop across the sea and then a car journey though Lewis leads to Harris by 9am. The two islands are joined together by a narrow isthmus of land. The border sign between the islands is a low-key affair: blink and you miss it. The main town of Tarbert then heralds the visitor's arrival in Harris.

For centuries, islanders on Lewis, Harris, and throughout the Outer Hebrides, have used traditional methods to produce "Clo Mor", or "the big cloth" that we have come to know as Harris Tweed. Its history is its fortune. Those who want a product with provenance are prepared to pay for it, not just for clothes but for furnishings, and accessories like shoes and bags. Harris Tweed, which is now fiercely protected by a 1993 Act of Parliament, is exported to 60 countries with Japan as the main international market. "The Japanese," says Margaret Ann MacLeod, Brand Director at Harris Tweed Hebrides, "are interested in authenticity."

Border sign approaching Harris from Lewis

Stornoway   Tarbert   Shawbost   Callanish   North Harris

It's not simple. There are no magic solutions. It took years with Harris Tweed. Fashion is fickle and we would have conferences and discussions about Harris Tweed and come up with handbags or once, a great idea for car seat covers. Can't remember why that didn't work. At one point, those in charge of the industry thought it was a material that should only be used for men's sports jackets. They didn't realise men weren't wearing sports jackets any more. Everything is of its time.

Iain Robertson,
HIE Chief Executive, 1991-2000

Margaret Ann MacLeod, from Harris Tweed Hebrides, at Shawbost Mill

The guarantee of that authenticity comes from the famous Orb trademark which has been stamped on Harris Tweed since 1911. Margaret, a friendly, articulate woman who can explain every stage of the complex processes the pure virgin wool goes through in the simplest of terms, points out a representative from the Harris Tweed Authority, the body which regulates the industry. "Look," she says above the clamour of the mill, "doesn't happen too often: a man with an iron." He is standing over a production line in the mill, checking the paperwork showing the source of the cloth and stamping the orb on with a transfer and steam iron every few metres.

Next door, in an adjoining showroom to the mill, pattern books from the 1960s are spread open across a table, while the history of Harris Tweed is displayed in original items hanging on a display rail. Past and present. A 1950s lady's coat in lavender tweed hangs on the rail, while a man's suit, in a special tweed produced for the 2014 Ryder cup, adorns a mannequin, the soft blues reminiscent of the seas and skies of the Outer Hebrides.

The fortunes of Harris Tweed have been cyclical but the story of its recent rejuvenation is a sign of the potential that the stunning group of islands known as the Western Isles, or the Outer Hebrides, has to be economically successful.

Production of the fabric reached a peak in the mid-1960s before entering a steep decline in the 70s and 80s and then an all-time low in 2009. The industry had become fragmented with no successful, coherent marketing and design policies. Against that background, Harris Tweed Hebrides was formed, a company that would seize the industry by the collar and lift it into a different place. The company re-established one of only three Harris Tweed mills in existence, a building which lay redundant but which still had some manufacturing equipment inside. Less than ten years after it was formed, Harris Tweed Hebrides now commands over 70% of the market share and has an annual turnover of £10 million.

Harris Tweed is known for the depth and intensity of its colour which is achieved by dying the wool at the fibre stage, then blending the vibrant wool to form unique yarn and colours before hand-weaving. The blend gives special flecks of colour that give light and texture to the fabric. Bottle green and lavender can run through moss green like heather across moorland. "There are 50 solid colour used in blend 'recipes'," explains Margaret, "We use around 150 yarn colours, and 600 patterns – but we have thousands."

The luxurious but hard wearing fabric is already a key contributor to the economy of the Outer Hebrides but it is estimated that by 2018, production will have increased by another 20%. In an economically fragile area, this is significant. It was always in areas like Lewis and Harris that the success of HIE would be judged. Population had been declining steadily for generations. But in the 2011 census, the population of the Outer Hebrides grew for just the second time since the 1970s.

Harris Tweed accounts for 56% of all manufacturing jobs on the island. Yet in 2009, the industry looked dead. One of the men who is generally regarded as having made a significant contribution to its revitalisation is Brian Wilson, the chairman of Harris Tweed Hebrides, founder of the West Highland Free Press and a former Scottish Office minister. He is not on the island when I visit, but later, we catch up in a plush hotel in Blythswood Square in Glasgow.

The population of the Outer Hebrides grew by 4.6% between the last two censuses. The man on the street wouldn't have expected that – but it did.

Alex Paterson,
HIE Chief Executive, 2010 to present

"Do you notice anything?" he asks. I hadn't, but on close inspection, the smart dark sofas we are sitting on are Harris Tweed. So are the dining chairs. And the lamps. Eight-thousand metres of Harris Tweed fabric were used in the hotel's interior with 25 different design patterns.

"I knew how critical it had been for decades to the economy of Lewis and Harris," explains Brian, who now lives on Lewis. "In government, I tried to help in any way I could." Brian and others on the island watched with disappointment as the industry declined. A friend of Brian's put money into buying the mill at Shawbost and together with Chief Executive Ian Angus Mackenzie they embarked on establishing the mill and Harris Tweed Hebrides was born.

Harris Tweed is synonymous with quality and luxury and many top established fashion designers are customers. Alexander McQueen. Yves St Laurent. Vivienne Westwood. Paul Smith. But the company also tried to look to the future of design. "We started working with young, edgy Scottish designers," explains Brian. The fabric retained its past but also acquired a future. The huntin', shootin' fishin' brigade still wanted tweed, but a new market opened up too. "Topman bought it and that's very important. Harris Tweed had disappeared from the British High Street but now it's got a second market."

Part of the reason the industry has been so critical to the Outer Hebrides is because the profits are not centralised in any one place. Weavers live all over the islands. "One of the things that is different about Harris Tweed is that it takes money into the villages,"

Brian Wilson, Chairman, Harris Tweed Hebrides

Stornoway   Tarbert   Shawbost   Callanish   North Harris

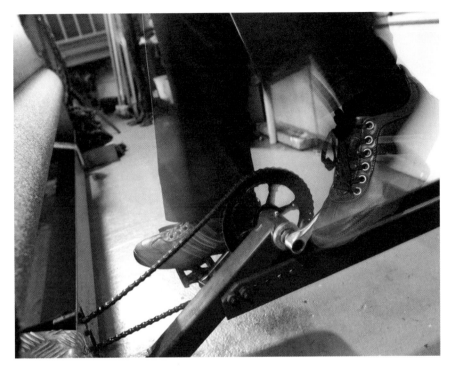

explains Brian. "If Harris Tweed is doing well, the islands are doing well…it's not just waged employment in Stornoway. It's very localised."

The production of the handwoven tweed known as Harris Tweed provides the main source of work within the private sector in the Outer Hebrides and it is vital to the economy of those islands that the integrity, distinctive character and worldwide renown of Harris Tweed should be maintained.

In this Act Harris Tweed means a tweed which has been handwoven by the islanders at their homes in the Outer Hebrides, finished in the Outer Hebrides, and made from pure new virgin wool dyed and spun in the Outer Hebrides.

1993 Act of Parliament

Top: Weaver pedalling the loom
Below: Horgabost beach on the Isle of Harris

On the outskirts of a comfortable housing estate in Stornoway, Neil Macleod is in his garage, door open, working on his prize machine. It's not a smart, glossy car. Nor is it a sleek, powerful motorbike. It's a Harris Tweed loom. Neil's feet work pedals much like a bike, cycling round and round to produce the cloth.
"It keeps me very fit," he says.

Over many years, HIE invested substantial sums in helping the industry move from single width to more economically viable double length looms. Neil got his second-hand for little over £2,000 but a brand new loom can cost a weaver £20,000. In return, a full-time weaver could earn up to £30-40,000 a year, a very significant salary in the economy of the Outer Hebrides.

The fact this is Neil's home is also significant. A key stipulation of the 1993 Act of Parliament is that Harris Tweed must be made at the home of the weaver using traditional methods. Neil was born in the rural South Lochs area of Lewis and his father had to leave the island to work in the sugar beet factory in Fife and in hydroelectric schemes all over Scotland. His mother used to send his father a box of island eggs and his father would send the box back full of sweets. Island ways were in Neil's blood and his

deepest ambition was to inherit one of the family's crofts. "Crofting is genetic," he says. "It runs through your veins."

He ran his own engineering business but retains the croft to this day. He's 69 and though he only turned to weaving nine years ago, he now trains other weavers. Weavers can earn attractive salaries but being their own bosses also offers attractive flexibility. "The versatility attracted me," says Neil. "I could do other things as well."

There's a sense of pride about Neil and his work that is deeply connected to these islands and the history of its product. "You never know who is going to wear the cloth you weave. It could appear on the catwalks of Milan or New York. It could be gracing some Russian oligarch.

It's a tremendous heritage. People are prepared to pay for the uniqueness of it."

The tweed, the crafting, the Gaelic, says Neil. His sense of identity is all wrapped up in those things. Even when he left the island to train, he never really thought he'd live anywhere else. He was always coming back. "There is a pull," he says. "Heritage… family… the poems, the songs. It's our make-up: the islander. The longing never leaves you."

Stornoway   Tarbert   Shawbost   Callanish   North Harris

Neil Macleod, weaver

Our main mission as I saw it was to create work so people could have an income and stay in their communities. If there was an area where it was difficult to get jobs going, you could invest in village halls and community enterprises that would get people involved in doing things in their area. If a business needed more support we could give a grant to train their workforce. There was always something we could do in each area for business and the community.

Iain Robertson,
HIE Chief Executive, 1991-2000

An Lanntair, multi-purpose arts centre, Stornoway

Stornoway   Tarbert   Shawbost   Callanish   North Harris

In a smart but minimalist office in Tarbert, Harris, Simon Erlanger is talking about his boss, Anderson Bakewell. Bakewell, an American born musicologist, began a love affair with Harris back in the 1960s. The island alternates between gentle rolling panoramas and austere, rocky lunar landscapes, but to Bakewell, this remote spot was the very centre of the universe. He wanted to give something back to the place he loved. The "something" has turned into Scotland's newest £11 million whisky distillery.

Simon, an urbane and smooth-talking former sales and marketing executive in the drinks industry was brought in to realise the dream. "I asked Anderson why

a distillery. "He said, 'I've always thought it would be great if you could drink this island. "The senses are very important here. The softness of the water, the landscape, the climate. Anderson Bakewell wanted to bottle the island and its people and bring it to the world."

It's a sentiment Simon can now understand. He lived in Switzerland before moving to Edinburgh 25 years ago and has worked for Glenmorangie and drinks giant Diageo. His holidays had been taken mainly in the west coast of Scotland but he had never ventured as far as the Outer Hebrides. When he did, like Bakewell he was smitten and agreed to spend five days a week here to establish the distillery.

"The people on Harris make it one of the most special places I've ever been to." What characterises the islanders? "They are amazing," he says. "Open, warm, incredibly hospitable and kind. But their overall perspective is adaptability, a can-do, hands-on attitude that is always about how to solve problems – perhaps because of the adversity they are used to."

The new Isle of Harris distillery will soon produce 100,000 litres of alcohol each year. On the wall of the office where we are sitting talking, is a statement of company values. "For, with, and from the Isle of Harris," it says. If Harris Tweed is one of the island's oldest industries, this is the newest. Both aim to underline

Isle of Harris Distillers, Tarbert

quality and exploit island history.
"We want to bring out this beautiful remote island's connection with Harris Tweed and quality and artisans. It's important to create something of quality that boosts tourism. We want to create something of pride for Harris that is also a catalyst for other initiatives of quality."

The distillery will produce The Hearach, a new single malt whose name means, "Man of Harris." There is no great technical mystery to making whisky but the water used in production is important. "This is a perfect location," says Simon. "The water is incredibly soft and is running over Lewisian gneiss rock that is 3 billion years old – some of the oldest rock on the planet. The bedrock of this ancient island is now creating water that feeds the distillery."

The site is an example of visionary planning. Long before distillery plans, the site was reclaimed from the sea by HIE and earmarked for future business development. Both HIE and the Scottish Government together invested over

£3 million in establishing the distillery, the biggest ever grant to a food and drink company. The money acted as a catalyst for private investment. But there is one snag for investors in a new whisky distillery. It takes ten years to produce a malt whisky so there is no fast buck to be made. To compensate, Isle of Harris Distillers will also distil Harris gin. "It's one way of generating early revenue," explains Simon.

"Our gin," he continues, "will have a Hebridean ingredient that has to be dived for: sugar kelp. It's a seaweed and very sweet when you distil it. It's a lovely ingredient that nobody else has ever had before and it's a way of linking Harris gin with the Hebrides."

Isle of Harris Distillers, Tarbert

Simon Erlanger, Isle of Harris Distillers

Kenny Maclean, Isle of Harris Distillers

The distillery will generate 20 jobs initially, a significant number for Harris. One of the new employees is Kenny Maclean, who lost his job when a local business folded. He's trained in electronics but like most islanders knows how to diversify. He has a croft, a couple of wind turbines, keeps pigs… now he makes whisky. He has a quiet manner but flashes of a dry, island sense of humour pepper his conversation and he delivers punchlines in such a deadpan way that there's a heartbeat before registering what he's just said. He looks out the window, quietly relishing the fact that he's missing a delivery because the boss has told him he can talk to me.

Kenny moved back to Harris in 2003 from Birmingham. What brought him back? "I've no idea," he says. "I ask myself that all the time. I was still single but I suppose I had partied myself out." He was spending four hours a day on the congested roads around Birmingham commuting to his job. And then each time he came back to Harris, he found it tugged increasingly at his heartstrings when he had to leave again, particularly watching his mother struggle alone to look after his grandfather.

"At 18 I couldn't wait to go. But for a certain type of person, at a certain stage of life, the islands have a lot to offer." He is married with children now and is content to stay. "I think if I went away again now, I'd think yes, but this is not what you should be doing Kenny. If a croft has been in your family for ten generations, you have respect for the people who went before you and a sense of duty to pass it on to your son. The croft is in a beautiful spot and it's as good a place as anywhere else in the world to be."

The islands seemed different to him when he returned. "There was no money when I was growing up," he says. "Apart from the fishermen who always told you what a terrible time they were having." He grins. "They were always driving round in new cars but they would never have admitted they were doing well."

For any remote area, the keys to survival are affordable housing and sustainable employment. For both local and incomer, the new distillery offers the kind of sustainable employment that enables them to make Harris their home. Simon would be content to make this his final career move. "To be given the opportunity to start something like this and lead it and make it a success…" he says with relish. He would stay here? "I would like to think this is me forever."

Callanish, Lewis. This is where there really is a sense of forever. The panoramic view sweeps across Loch Roag and the hills of the island of Great Bernera. Through a gate, on the mound of a hill, tourists straggle across the striking arrangement

of ancient standing stones that form an inner circle of 13 stones with five avenues running from it like spokes on a wheel. The Callanish stones date back to around 2900 BC and are the oldest in the United Kingdom, older even than Stonehenge.

Like the rock that the Harris distillery's water runs over, they are made of Lewisian gneiss. Their significance is the subject of speculation but it would seem that this remote corner on the west coast of Lewis, where there is little but a meeting of the sea and the sky and the hills, was once a place of great importance. The arrangement of seemingly haphazard sized stones suggest it was a centre for prehistoric religious activity. And it makes you think out here on a cloudy summer's day, as a few splodges of rain begin to hit the stones, that it doesn't matter how tiny or remote a place, how isolated or challenging its environment, 'everywhere' can be an important 'somewhere' when it offers something unique.

The uniqueness of the Outer Hebrides has perhaps not always appealed to its young people, though some return later in life. A Skills Investment Plan published in 2015 highlights the "missing generation" of young people who have moved out of the area and the fact that 20% of 16-24 year olds who stay are unemployed.

In the tearoom and visitor centre attached to the Callanish site, Anna Mackay is working in her first full-time job as a temporary employee in design and marketing after graduating from university with a degree in languages. Her post is supported by HIE. She spent a year in Spain and a year in France, but has returned home to the island of Great Bernera which is joined to Lewis by a bridge. It takes her only 15 minutes to drive from Bernera to Callanish, 30 minutes to Lewis's main town of Stornoway.

Stornoway   Tarbert   Shawbost   Callanish   North Harris

Anna is young, lively, pretty. Around 70% of her friends moved away and haven't come back, she admits. So what can this place offer her and her friends who are only in their twenties? "We're quite boring," she smiles. "We go hill walking like middle aged people." But, she adds, people pay a lot of money to go hillwalking and surfing in other places. The Outer Hebrides has it on tap, is like a giant outdoor playground.

Will she stay? She hesitates. She is not sure. "There's push and pull." Jobs and housing are the big issues and Anna currently lives with her parents. What's the pull? "The environment, the scenery, the peace and quiet, the chilled pace of life, the security. You know everyone. You feel safe here and a lot of people want that after living in the city."

The hills of home are visible from her office window. It is a comfortingly familiar sight but change could be imminent. The community there are waiting to hear if they will undergo the kind of transformation that has happened all over other parts of the Outer Hebrides: a community buy-out. If anything has changed the nature of land management and ownership across these islands, it is that.

Anna Mackay,
Callanish Visitor Centre

One of the most significant things HIE has done in creating long-term success is encourage land reform and community ownership of assets. Almost 70% of people in the Outer Hebrides now live in community owned land. It gives people the ability to drive their own future.

Willy Roe,
HIE Chairman, 2004-2012

In the offices of the North Harris Trust in Harris, Calum MacKay's healthy, weathered complexion and casual polo shirt make you think he's an outdoor worker. A shepherd, perhaps, or a gamekeeper. He's not, though his father was a ghillie. In fact Calum has just retired as a Gaelic teacher and deputy head of Sir E Scott School, but he does spend most of his time in the outdoors. He owns a croft, a boat for the fishing, and keeps sheep, tending to them all himself even when he worked at the local school.

"I wouldn't survive a week in the city," he says. "I need to be outside. I don't understand people who go home and watch telly from 5pm – 11pm. I can't understand people who live here and don't go outdoors."

His father worked on the North Harris Estate and Calum was recently asked to chair the community group that steered the estate into community ownership back in 2003. In his father's day, North Harris Estate was 65,000 acres of sporting land with a spectacular Atlantic coastline and Amhuinnsuidhe Castle at its heart. It's an area of outstanding natural beauty where deer roam and eagles soar over its mountain ranges. At the time of the sale, it was owned by Jonathan Bulmer of the Bulmer cider family. A businessman from Stoke-on-Trent, Ian Scar-Hall, who already owned a house locally, bought the castle and sporting rights. The community bought the land.

The first community buy-outs in the 1990s and early 2000s were high profile: Assynt Crofters Trust, Eigg, then North Harris. The idea has become increasingly common with 67% of people in the Outer Hebrides now living on community

Calum MacKay,
Chairman, North Harris Trust

owned land. For North Harris, it has been a real success with local people running the estate and managing the assets. "The opportunity presented itself at the right time," says Calum MacKay. "The principal reason was to give people ownership, involvement and pride in their own community. That has definitely increased."

North Harris Trust was in a fortunate position. The community had enjoyed a good relationship with the owner, Jonathan Bulmer, and negotiations to buy the land were amicable.

Historically, land ownership is an important and sensitive subject for Highlanders. The 19th century clearances that saw crofters swept from the land might be a long time ago, but the repercussions have echoed through the years since. For HIE it has not been a narrow political issue, but one which falls within their remit of social development. The lives of ordinary people, their ability to eke out a living in geographically remote and challenging areas, were at the mercy of powerful landowners, some of whom were supportive of their communities and some of whom were not. Something had to change.

Iain Robertson, Chief Executive of HIE from 1991-2000, pinpoints when it did. It was 1997 and Tony Blair's Labour government had just been elected. Dr Jim Hunter, historian and land reform campaigner, was about to take over as Chairman at HIE. "We were asked by the then Scottish Office if we could do something about land ownership," recalls Robertson. "I said yep, we could." The result was the Community Land Unit which came into being in 1997.

[Land reform] was a boost to confidence. It was utilising resources. It was encouraging and enabling and it created a lot of opportunity.

Jim Hunter,
HIE Chairman, 1998- 2004

"Communities got tired of another unknown landlord coming in," explains John Watt, now Chairman of the Scottish Land Fund and former Director of Strengthening Communities at HIE. "They could get someone who invested and was great – or someone who wanted the land as a personal playground. With community ownership, people were able to do their own development rather than waiting for development to be done to them.

HIE's Community Land Unit, though, did not simply arise out of nowhere. The threads led back through a number of important initiatives. From the start, HIDB, and then HIE, had a social remit. Developing communities has always been at the heart of their strategy. Methods to enable this evolved through the co-operative movement which had begun in Ireland and was replicated in the Highlands and Islands. Today, this has developed into social enterprises. There is a common concept running through all of it: ordinary people can come together to effectively manage community assets.

In 2002, when North Harris came up for sale, the Land Reform (Scotland) Act was progressing through the new Scottish Parliament. This would allow a rural community the right to register an interest in land and have first option to buy if it went up for sale. The North Harris Trust needed £2.2 million to buy the land. The money was raised through the Scottish Land Fund and HIE, who also offered

invaluable support and advice. The result is that the people of North Harris now manage their own affairs. But it's more than that. "We don't just manage the land. We do try to develop business and tourism. We are pro-active," says Calum MacKay.

The trust employs eight staff who oversee the management of the deer stock, fish farm leases, wind turbines and hydro projects. It is now an established community enterprise and makes enough money to plough some back directly into the community through a development fund which individuals and businesses can apply to. The trust also exercised its social and charitable remit by working with a local housing association to build new, affordable housing on the island for locals.

Crucially, community ownership has changed the nature of people's relationship with the land in the Highlands and Islands. "When I was young," says Calum MacKay, "It was the factor in the castle who made the decisions. Older people in particular, who had grown up with the situation of absentee landlords on typical highland estates, didn't see how a group of local people could run the estate. It had been this way for 150 years and they thought that was just the way Highland estates were run."

"Now," continues Calum, "everyone feels involved." Community ownership means people are no longer at the mercy

Angling on Loch Bhoisimid (also Voshimid) on
the Amhuinnsuidhe Castle Estate

David Wright, Horshader Community Development, during construction of the community wind turbine

Stornoway   Tarbert   Shawbost   Callanish   North Harris

of individual landowners to manage and develop their employment, housing and communities. They can forge their own path. "There is a sense of ownership," says Calum MacKay. "You have to create it – it doesn't just happen – I think we have been quite good at doing that. People here are really dedicated."

It's not just the land of North Harris that the trust now controls but its water and wind. 2015 saw the construction of a hydroelectric project at Bunavoneader, next to the remains of a 100-year-old whaling station, and the development of a three-turbine wind farm at nearby Monan Hill, which is expected to bring in £1 million over the 20-year life of the project. These renewable energy projects are part of a wider Highlands and Islands-wide community energy movement, where local people are investing in solar, wind, hydro and biomass schemes to heat village halls, power social housing and, like North Harris, bring in real long-term income for wider community benefit.

Encouraged by then Chairman, Jim Hunter, HIE established a Community Energy Unit in 2002 to support and stimulate local use of the region's outstanding renewable energy potential. In 2008, this became an independent organisation, Community Energy Scotland (CES), which developed projects such as a hydrogen powered car in Unst, Shetland, and a three-turbine wind farm in Gigha known locally as the "dancing ladies". The Isle of Eigg was supported by HIE and CES to build a completely new electricity network for the island, powered by renewable energy, replacing the island's noisy and expensive diesel generators. Owning and accessing the land, and being able to harvest its natural resources for heat and light, has transformed

Local people are now in control. They can't say it's the laird not looking after them. They ARE the laird. They control their own destiny.

Sandy Cumming,
HIE Chief Executive, 2000-2010

islands and communities across the Highlands and Islands. Indeed, this model of community support, instigated by HIE, has now been adopted across the whole of Scotland.

Through the window of the plane back to Inverness, the islands spread below, glowing like hidden secret jewels in the evening light. "Who owns this landscape? Has owning anything to do with love?" Norman MacCaig speculated in his poem, "A Man in Assynt." In North Harris, at least, it would seem it does. The land lasts longer than all of us, enduring beyond the lives of individuals. In that sense, it is, as MacCaig noted, "masterless". No man can truly be a possessor of land - only a temporary caretaker. It is the spirit of that principle that HIE has consistently recognised and encouraged, a spirit that offers these remote islands a way forward for the future.

Who owns this landscape?
The millionaire who bought it
Or the poacher staggering downhill in the early morning
With a deer on his back?

A Man in Assynt,
Norman MacCaig

Stornoway   Tarbert   Shawbost   Callanish   North Harris

Amhuinnsuidhe Castle

Where next?

There are differences across the Highlands and Islands. We have to be careful not to be Inverness-centric.

Lorne Crerar,
HIE Chairman, 2012 to present

What would the Highlands and Islands be like without HIDB and HIE? I definitely believe it would have been different. How can you prove that? You can't. But in my view you just need to look at the number of projects over years and years that HIE helped with.

Sir Fraser Morrison,
HIE Chairman, 1992-1998

It is hard to separate the 'what is' from the 'what might have been'. But if we are looking for a measure of growth in the Highlands and Islands, the population figures tell an important story. Depopulation was one of the most significant and intransigent problems facing the area in the 1960s when the population was at a record low of 380,866. Fifty years later, it stands at almost 470,000.

The Inner Moray Firth, which takes in Inverness and stretches from south Ross-shire to Badenoch and Strathspey, is the most densely populated area of the region. Taking in the city of Inverness, and towns like Dingwall, Alness and Aviemore, its population has grown by almost 15% since 2001 and its unemployment rate is below the national average. The Highlander living in the Inner Moray Firth is no longer on anybody's conscience.

But that is not the whole picture. The comparative affluence of the Inner Moray Firth is not reflected everywhere in the Highlands and Islands. The first chairman of HIDB, Sir Robert Grieve, made clear that the organisation would not be considered successful until it had transformed the peripheral, most economically challenging, areas of the region like the Outer Hebrides. "No matter what success is achieved in the eastern or central Highlands," he said, "the Board will be judged by its ability to hold population in the true crofting areas."

There are almost 100 inhabited islands in the region which enrich its distinctive nature but which pose particular challenges in terms of transport and industry. The Isle of Skye has been one of the success stories in these more economically challenging areas. The Outer Hebrides, an ethereally beautiful but remote part of the Highlands and Islands, has been harder to support. But even there, positive change is beginning to ripple through the islands like a gentle spring breeze. At the last census, the population grew for the first time by 4.6%. A number of significant businesses have grown up there, including the internationally renowned company BASF Pharma on the Isle of Lewis, a chemical company that produces Omega-3 oils.

The coastline at Yesnaby at dusk, Mainland Orkney

> *HIE and its partners haven't succeeded so far in turning around the fortunes of all parts of the region. If it was easy, we would have done it. Until we do, we will not be able to say, 'job done'.*
>
> **Jim Hunter,**
> HIE Chairman, 1998-2004

But it is not 'job done' for Highlands and Islands Enterprise. There is still much to be achieved to ensure economic stability and thriving communities in the more fragile corners of the region, not just in the Outer Hebrides but in mainland areas like Caithness and Sutherland and the more remote areas of Argyll. It is not just about propping up individual businesses with grants. It's about creating the social infrastructure that creates sustainable communities. With support, these areas can be viable but it will require initiative, determination and imagination.

The 'Highland problem' Willie Ross referred to when he set up HIDB in the 1960s was obvious to all who didn't turn their heads away. Something needed to be done and HIDB was that 'something'. It was given the most extensive powers of any UK state development agency and it created real change. It would be ironic if that success was now seen to make its existence less necessary. Perhaps the truth is that the Highlands and Islands will always need special treatment. For as long as the distinctive magic of this area remains – its remote, sparsely populated nature, its challenging physical terrain, its unique language and culture – it will require extra effort and support to keep it alive.

Dunnet Head Lighthouse perched on dramatic cliffs, Caithness

There's more to be done everywhere — even in Inverness. Our aim is not just to address problems. It's saying, where are the opportunities? And then going hard after them.

Alex Paterson,
HIE Chief Executive, 2010 to present

The nature of HIE's work may have changed and developed. It may no longer be about breathing life into a dying patient, about resuscitating quickly before the last painful gasp. But it is still about ensuring its future prosperity. It's about creating and maintaining a vision for a richly diverse area that contains everything from the city of Inverness to the stunningly remote, ivory-sanded beauty of South Uist. A vision of a thriving, socially secure and economically vibrant region that just happens to also be one of the most beautiful in the world.

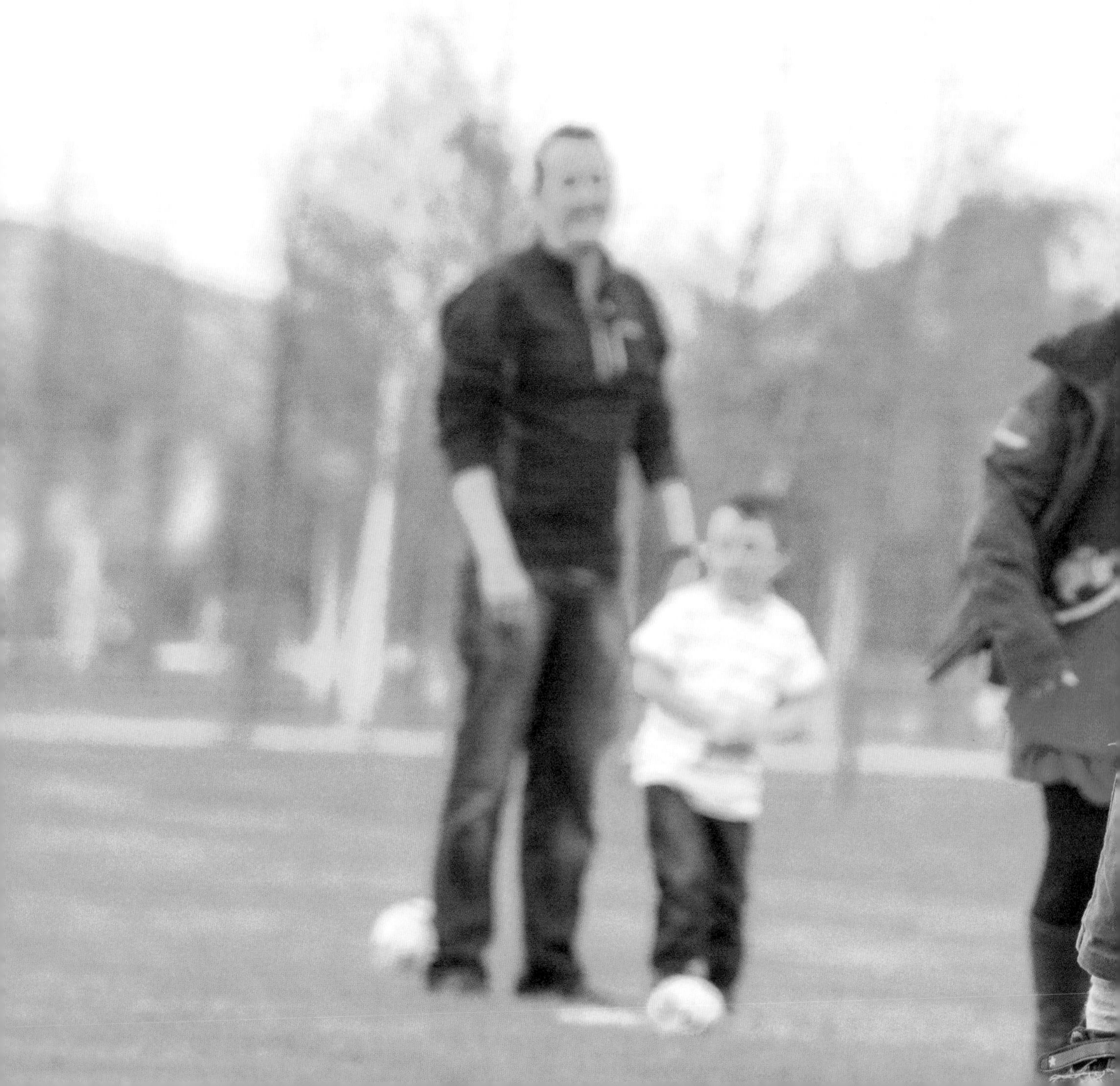

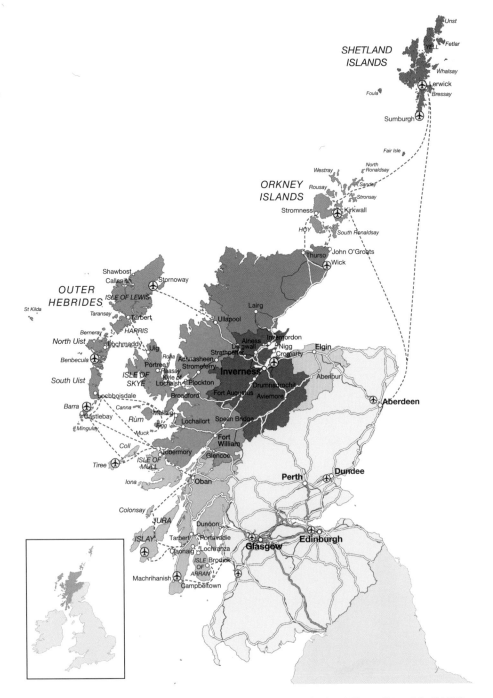

SHETLAND
ISLANDS

Unst
Fetlar
YELL
Whalsay
Foula
Lerwick
Bressay
Sumburgh

Fair Isle

Westray
North
Ronaldsay
Rousay
Sanday
ORKNEY
ISLANDS
Stronsay
Stromness
Kirkwall

HOY
South Ronaldsay

John O'Groats
Thurso
Wick

OUTER
HEBRIDES

Shawbost
Callanish
Stornoway
ISLE OF LEWIS
St Kilda
Lairg
Taransay
Tarbert
Ullapool
Berneray
HARRIS
North Uist
Lochmaddy
Uig
Alness
Invergordon
Benbecula
Rona
Achnasheen
Dingwall
Elgin
Portree
Strathpeffer
Nigg
Raasay
Stromeferry
Cromarty
ISLE OF
SKYE
Kyle of
Lochalsh
Plockton
Inverness
Aberlour
South Uist
Drumnadrochit
Broadford
Fort Augustus
Aviemore
Lochboisdale
Canna
Barra
Mallaig
Aberdeen
Castlebay
Rùm
Lochailort
Speap Bridge
Egg
Mingulay
Muck
Fort
William
Coll
Tobermory
Glencoe
Tiree
ISLE OF
MULL
Iona
Oban
Perth
Dundee
Colonsay
JURA
Dunoon
ISLAY
Tarbert
Portavadie
Edinburgh
Claonaig
Lochranza
Glasgow
ISLE
Brodick
Machrihanish
OF
ARRAN
Campbeltown